# Practical Planetary Magick

## Acknowledgements

*This book is dedicated to the Peacock Angel, Helene Hodge.*
*A true weaver of the webs of the wandering stars.*

We would like to take this opportunity to thank Joseph Peterson for his kind permission to reproduce his copies of images from Giordano Bruno's book, *De Imaginum Compositione* (1591), from his superb website www.esotericarchives.com. These images adorn Chapter 3 of this book. Thank you, as always, to the staff the British Library in London for always being professional, helpful and friendly. Thank you to Stephen Skinner for his ongoing support, encouragement and input on our projects.

Finally, our thanks also to the alumni of the O.I.F. for their work, insights, their fraternity and ongoing support over the years.
*The light of Truth, burns with an Ineffable Flame.*

# About the Authors

Sorita d'Este & David Rankine are students and practitioners of the Western Esoteric Tradition who live and work in Wales (UK). This volume, their fifth book together, brings together their shared passion for planetary and ceremonial work. Both of them have lectured extensively on a wide range of esoteric subjects and have facilitated workshops throughout the UK and Europe. They first met in Atlantis Bookshop, London in 1999, it wasn't quite love at first sight, but when they met again in 2000 (again in that most magickal of bookshops in London), they decided to go and have a fruit smoothie and the rest as they say is "history"! In their work together they draw from their experience in a number of traditions, with their extensive research on a wide range of western esoteric subjects including Qabalah, Classical Paganism of Greece, Rome and Egypt, British & other "Celtic" mythologies – as well as that of the grimoire traditions (of course!)

You are welcome to write the authors:

Sorita d'Este & David Rankine

c/o BM Avalonia, London, WC1N 3XX, United Kingdom

For more information on their work see: www.avalonia.co.uk

# Practical Planetary Magick

**Working the Magick of the Classical Planets in the Western Mystery Tradition**

**David Rankine & Sorita d'Este**

Published by Avalonia

BM Avalonia
London
WC1N 3XX
England, UK

www.avaloniabooks.co.uk

PRACTICAL PLANETARY MAGIC

ISBN (10) 1-905297-01-7
ISBN (13) 978-1-905297-01-6

First Edition 2007
Design by Satori

# Other Books by the Authors

Sorita d'Este & David Rankine are the authors, or co-authors of the following published books:

**Celtic / British Mythology & Folklore**

The Isles of the Many Gods, 2007

The Guises of the Morrígan, 2005

**Greek Mythology, Magick & History**

Hekate: Keys to the Crossroads (Edited by Sorita d'Este), 2006

Artemis, Virgin Goddess of the Sun & Moon (by Sorita d'Este), 2005

**Egyptian Mysteries**

Heka: The Practices of Ancient Egyptian Ritual & Magic (by David Rankine), 2006

**Qabalah**

Climbing the Tree of Life (by David Rankine), 2005

**Source Works of Ceremonial Magic**

*(Stephen Skinner & David Rankine)*

Volume I – The Practical Angel Magic of Dr John Dee's Enochian Tables, 2004

Volume II – The Keys to the Gateway of Magic, 2005

Volume III – The Goetia of Dr Rudd, 2007

**Other / Practical Magick**

Avalonia's Book of Chakras, 2006

Circle of Fire, 2005

Becoming Magick, 2004 (by David Rankine)

Crystals Healing & Folklore, 2002 (by David Rankine)

Magick Without Peers, 1997 (David Rankine & Ariadne Rainbird)

# Table of Contents

Planetary Magick ........ 13

The Seven Wandering Stars ........ 17
The Sun - Works of Wealth ........ 18
Mercury - Works of Mind ........ 20
Venus - Works of Beauty ........ 22
The Moon - Works of Mystery ........ 24
Mars - Works of Power ........ 26
Jupiter - Works of Expansion ........ 29
Saturn - Works of Form ........ 32

The Planetary Deities ........ 35
The Solar God ........ 37
The Mercurial God ........ 39
The Venusian Goddess ........ 41
The Lunar Goddess ........ 43
The Martial God ........ 45
The Jupiterian God ........ 47
The Saturnian God ........ 49

Meditation Journeys ........ 51
Journey to the God Sol ........ 53
Journey to the God Mercury ........ 55
Journey to the Goddess Venus ........ 57
Journey to the Goddess Luna ........ 59
Journey to the God Mars ........ 61
Journey to the God Jupiter ........ 63
Journey to the God Saturn ........ 65

Planetary Days & Hours ........ 67
Planetary Days ........ 69
Planetary Hours ........ 70

Invocation & Evocation ........ 76

The Olympic Spirits ........ 80
Invoking the Olympic Spirits ........ 88

Qabalistic Spirits ........ 94
The Spiritual Creatures of the Sun ........ 99
The Spiritual Creatures of Mercury ........ 101
The Spiritual Creatures of Venus ........ 103
The Spiritual Creatures of the Moon ........ 105
The Spiritual Creatures of Mars ........ 108
The Spiritual Creatures of Jupiter ........ 110
The Spiritual Creatures of Saturn ........ 112
Planetary Intelligences ........ 114
Manifestation of Spiritual Creatures ........ 115

Kamea Sigilisation ........ 116

Amulets & Talismans ........ 122
Consecration Ritual ........ 126

Preparation ........ 129

The Magick Circle ........ 133
Planetary Circle (Subtle) ........ 134
Planetary Circle (Physical) ........ 136

The Ritual of the Heptagram....138

Planetary Pyramids....141
The Solar Pyramid....142
The Mercurial Pyramid....145
The Venusian Pyramid....149
The Lunar Pyramid....153
The Martial Pyramid....156
The Jupiterian Pyramid....159
The Saturnian Pyramid....162

The Trans-Saturnian Planets....165
Uranus....166
Neptune....168
Pluto....170

Angle Webs....172

APPENDIX....175
Inter-Planetary Relationships....176
The Kameas....177
Sigils for Planetary Intelligences & Spirits....183
a. Kamea Sigils for the Seven Archangels....183
b. Kamea Sigils for the Planetary Intelligences....186
c. Kamea Sigils of the Planetary Spirits....188
Hebrew Names....191
Planetary Fragrances....195
The Planets and Minerals....197
The Planets and Plants....199
The Planets & Mankind....200
The Planets and Animals....201

Planetary Sigils....................202
Planetary Contemplations....................206
Invocation of Planetary Intelligences....................209
The Heptagram....................212
Terms & Definitions....................214

Bibliography....................216

**CHAPTER 1**

# Planetary Magick

*"The wheel of the stars goes forth with seven wheels of seven planets. They are Saturn, Jupiter, Mars, the Sun, Venus, Mercury, and the Moon."*[1]

The influence of the planets subtly surrounds us all the time, in the names of the days of the week. In myths from around the world, we find repeated examples of the seven-fold symbolism and importance that was placed on the influence of the planets on everyday life.

When working with the planets, we are raising our gazes to the stars, setting our sights beyond the horizon of the next hill or boundary. As was said in the Orphic mysteries of ancient Greece, *"We are children of earth and starry heaven"*. Exploring the mysteries associated with the planets helps us to reach up into the heavens whilst keeping our feet firmly rooted on the ground.

The ancients saw the planets as being extremely important to the lives of mankind. The planets represent the higher powers of the universe beyond the Earth. For this reason when you do planetary work, you are bringing the stellar force to earth to empower your magick appropriately, applying the principle of *"As above, so below"*.

Today the most common use of planetary magick seems to be for the creation of amulets and talismans. This field of planetary magick has a rich history of practice from ancient Greece through to the Middle Ages and Renaissance through to the current day, and is covered in the chapter on Amulets & Talismans. However it is only one area of planetary magick, and Theurgy and Invocation and Evocation also form an important part of the

---

1 Sepher Rezial Hemelach, p118.

practices of planetary magick, as will be seen from the material contained within this volume.

Theurgy is a term which has fallen somewhat out of use, although the principle it represents has not. Theurgy represents the quest for the perfection of the gods through identification with their perfected divine qualities. Devotional work with deities, including the use of hymns, and meditation journeys which include an interaction with deity are all Theurgic techniques. Theurgy is further discussed in the chapters on Planetary Deities and Meditation Journeys.

As a large component of planetary magick involves working with spiritual creatures, the logical question to ask has to be, what are the benefits of working with different types of spiritual creatures? The reasons and benefits for working with different types of spiritual creature need to be considered within the context of the material and techniques we have presented, and this is done in the chapters on Invocation & Evocation, Planetary Deities and on Qabalistic Spirits.

Table of Ritual Intentions

The intent of a ceremony will determine its nature. To ensure a successful ceremony requires a precise intent and focused appropriate energy. This table gives the appropriate planets for a wide range of intentions in a convenient form for easy access.

| **Intention** | **Planet** |
|---|---|
| Ambition, development of | Jupiter |
| Anger, controlling | Mars |
| Astral travel | Moon |
| Attraction, increasing | Venus |
| Beauty, developing | Venus |
| Birth, safely | Moon |
| Business success | Mercury |
| Career success | Jupiter or Sun |
| Clairvoyance, developing | Moon |

| Intention | Planet |
|---|---|
| Communication, improving | Mercury |
| Courage, enhancing | Mars |
| Creativity, increasing | Venus |
| Discord, causing | Mars |
| Discord, preventing | Mercury |
| Dreams, promoting and remembering | Moon |
| Duty, performing | Saturn |
| Energy, increasing | Mars |
| Enthusiasm, increasing | Jupiter |
| Equilibrium, establishing | Saturn |
| Ethics, developing | Jupiter |
| Examination study | Saturn |
| Examination success | Mercury |
| Fear, dispelling | Mars |
| Fertility, increasing | Venus |
| Flexibility, developing | Mercury |
| Fortune, improving | Jupiter |
| Friendship, developing | Venus |
| Future, learning the | Moon or Mercury |
| Glamour, developing | Moon |
| Harmony, developing | Sun |
| Healing, giving | Sun |
| Health, improving | Jupiter or Sun |
| Home, protecting | Saturn |
| Honour, acquiring | Jupiter |
| Humour, improving | Jupiter |
| Illusions, creating | Moon |
| Illusions, dispelling | Saturn |
| Influence, developing | Mercury |
| Journey, protection | Mercury (land, air) or Moon (sea) |
| Knowledge, increasing | Mercury |

| **Intention** | **Planet** |
|---|---|
| Law, dealing with | Jupiter or Saturn |
| Leadership, developing | Sun or Jupiter |
| Love, obtaining or promoting | Venus |
| Luck, improving | Jupiter |
| Lust, satisfying | Venus |
| Memory, improving | Mercury |
| Money, acquiring | Sun |
| Music, improving or learning | Mercury |
| Passion, increasing | Venus or Mars |
| Patience, developing | Saturn |
| Patronage, obtaining | Sun |
| Peace, establishing | Sun or Mercury |
| Pleasure, ensuring | Venus |
| Practicality, developing | Saturn |
| Promotion, gaining | Sun or Jupiter |
| Property, recovering | Mercury |
| Public Speaking, successfully | Mercury |
| Responsibility, taking | Jupiter |
| Self-confidence, increasing | Venus |
| Self-discipline, developing | Saturn |
| Sex-drive, decreasing | Saturn |
| Sex-drive, increasing | Mars |
| Social skills, improving | Venus |
| Strength, increasing | Mars |
| Teaching, developing | Saturn |
| Truth, learning or promoting | Jupiter |
| Unconscious, accessing | Moon |
| Vigour, increasing | Mars |
| Wealth, improving | Sun or Jupiter |
| Willpower, strengthening | Sun |

**CHAPTER 2**

# The Seven Wandering Stars

*"We are also to show forth, what Divine, gifts, powers & Virtues, man receiveth from the celestial bodies (that is) the seven planets; called by the Astrologers the seven erratic or wandering Stars."*[2]

The influence of the seven classical *"planets"* or *"wandering stars"* has been one of the central mysteries of spiritual traditions since the people of the city states of the first civilization of Sumeria gazed at the heavens around seven thousand years ago. Their astrologers, artisans and priests created the first known alphabet (cuneiform) alongside arithmetic and astronomy. From this cradle of invention also came the first calendar.

The Sumerians identified the five *"stars"* that wandered through the night sky, which we know today as the planets Mercury, Venus, Mars, Jupiter and Saturn. Together with the two luminaries of the Sun and Moon, they attributed these seven *"wandering stars"* to some of their most important deities, and the connection between the heavenly gods and their influence on the earthly realm of man was laid out as a template for future cultures to learn from and refine.

So here we present the seven wandering stars, or deathless powers as the Greeks called them, still illuminating the darkness with their wisdom and inspiration for mankind as they have done for many thousands of years past. Through time and space the planets exert their influence, and by working with them we can align ourselves more effectively with the subtle powers of change which surround us at all times through our lives.

---

2 Janua Magica Reserata.

# The Sun - Works of Wealth

*"From the Sun Nobleness of mind perspicuity of Judgement & Imagination, the nature of Knowledge & opinion, Maturity, Counsel, Zeal, Light of Justice, Reason & judgement to Distinguish Right from wrong purging Light from the Darkness of Ignorance, the Glory of truth found out, & Charity the mother & Queen of all Virtues."*[3]

| | |
|---|---|
| **Numbers** | 6, 36, 216, 666 |
| **Colour** | Gold, Orange, Yellow |
| **Rules** | Leo |
| **Metal** | Gold |
| **Day of the Week** | Sunday |
| **Element** | Fire |
| **Direction** | South |
| **Concepts** | Advancement, Dominance, Egotism, Friendship, Greed, Healing, Illumination, Individuality, Joy, Leadership, Personal Power, Success, Wealth, Will |
| **Tools** | Cymbals, Lamen, Lance, Rose Cross, Sword |
| **Deities** | Apollo, Baal, Belenus, Gráinne, Helios, Lugh, Mithras, Re (Ra), Sekhmet, Shamash, Sol |
| **Archangel** | Michael |

3 The Keys to the Gateway of Magic.

The Sun is the centre of our universe, and is the giver of life through its light and heat, so it is unsurprising that it should have been such a central object of human fascination and worship for so many thousands of years. The Sun represents spiritual power, the heart or centre, the radiation of energy. It also embodies the idea of consciousness, the reality of the soul and spirit. The massive size of the Sun means it comprises more than 99% of the mass of our solar system, giving justification to the heliocentric nature of so many world religions.

With its connections to power, the association between the Sun, royalty and wealth are obvious. Hence the Sun has become known as the planet for advancement and success. The drive to succeed is accompanied by a strong will, and this is an essential quality for any spiritual path.

That friendship is associated with the Sun may seem surprising until you consider the illuminating and life-giving qualities of the Sun. Like the Sun, a true friendship adds light and joy and growth to our lives.

Sunlight itself helps us feel more positive and joyous. Without enough sunlight we can feel less motivated and positive, manifesting in many people as S.A.D. (Seasonal Affectiveness Disorder).

The importance of sunlight for life is also seen in the plant kingdom in the process of photosynthesis. Without the plants on land and phytoplankton in the sea, the entire food chain would break down. The Sun truly is the giver of life to the Earth!

Of course everything with a positive side tends to have a negative side as well. Too much light can be harmful and as with all things a balance is needed. The Earth herself provides the balance through her daily rotation, ensuring we experience the regular cycle of day and night (in most of the world).

Negative solar qualities include insatiable ambition, boastfulness, imperiousness, pride and tyranny. These can all be overcome by working with the positive solar qualities, and striving for balance in our actions, so we are not overcome by the harshness of too much light.

# Mercury - Works of Mind

*"From Mercury a piercing faith & belief, Clear reasoning, the Vigour of Interpreting & pronouncing, Gravity of speech, Acuteness of will, Discourse of Reason, & the swift motion of the Sincere."*[4]

| | |
|---|---|
| **Numbers** | 8, 64, 88, 888 |
| **Colour** | Orange, Light Blue |
| **Rules** | Gemini, Virgo |
| **Metal** | Mercury, Aluminium |
| **Day of the Week** | Wednesday |
| **Element** | Air |
| **Direction** | East |
| **Concepts** | Business, Communication, Deception, Flexibility, Healing, Hyperactivity, Insight, Magick, Memory, Music, Poetry, Protection, Psychopomp, Science, Speed, Theft, Travel, Trickery |
| **Tools** | Apron, Words, Caduceus |
| **Deities** | Hermes, Mercury, Nebu, Thoth, Zalmoxis |
| **Archangel** | Raphael |

4 The Keys to the Gateway of Magic.

Mercury is the smallest planet, closest to the Sun and orbiting it every 88 days. The ancient Greeks initially associated Mercury with Apollo in the morning and Hermes in the evening, and subsequently called it *Stilbon,* meaning *"the gleaming one"*. The Babylonians named Mercury after Nebu, their messenger god.

Mercury is associated with various qualities, like communication and trickery, both useful qualities when you are the messenger of the gods! And of course other qualities are also connected to Mercury and communication, like commerce and music.

Mercury has come to be connected with healing; bearing what is now called the caduceus. The original caduceus was a rod with a single snake curled around it, but it has become the accepted norm to call the winged rod with twin serpents as borne by the Greek God Hermes and Goddess Iris and adopted by the medical profession, the caduceus. Skill and knowledge are combined in healing, making it the Mercury skill par excellence.

The power of the mind and ideas, expressed through words, are all Mercurial qualities, and this can be seen as the process of magickal realisation. The quicksilver firing of ideas through our synapses into voiced reality perfectly embodies the fleet footed Mercury.

With its association to all things of the mind, one of the major Mercurial attributions is that of memory. And memory is an important skill for the art and practice of magick and all other skills.

Mercury is the psychopomp, the guide between the worlds. This role expresses the fluid quality of Mercury, the ability to adapt to one's environment and be at home in any surroundings and circumstances. It also brings in another quality of Mercury, that of protection when travelling.

Negative Mercurial traits are deceit, gossip, lying, and treachery. These qualities are all associated with communication, and can all be overcome with positive Mercurial traits.

# Venus - Works of Beauty

*"From Venus a fervent Love, most sweet hope, the Motion of Desire, order, Beauty, Sweetness, Desire of Increasing & propagation of it self."*[5]

| | |
|---|---|
| **Numbers** | 7, 49, 343, 777 |
| **Colour** | Green, Pink |
| **Rules** | Taurus, Libra |
| **Metal** | Copper |
| **Day of the Week** | Friday |
| **Element** | Earth |
| **Direction** | Centre |
| **Concepts** | Attraction, Art, Beauty, Culture, Emotions, Fertility, Grace, Inspiration, Jealousy, Love, Passion, Pleasure, Self-Confidence, Sensuality, Sexuality, Sociability |
| **Tools** | Belt, Girdle, Harp, Necklace |
| **Deities** | Aphrodite, Astarte, Hathor, Inanna, Ishtar, Lucifer, Venus |
| **Archangel** | Uriel |

5 The Keys to the Gateway of Magic.

Venus is the second closest planet to the Sun, and the nearest in size to the Earth, her neighbour. Venus is the brightest planetary body in the night sky after the Moon, the first to be seen in the evening (as *"the evening star"*) and the last to be seen before the dawn (as *"the morning star"*).

The Babylonians knew Venus by the name of the goddess Ishtar, and the ancient Greeks associated the planet Venus with Aphrodite and knew it as *Phosphorus*, meaning *"the light bearer"*, and *Hesperos*, meaning *"the dusk star"*. The name of Phosphorus was also associated by the Greeks with the goddess Hekate, and her twin torches may be seen to symbolise Venus as the morning and evening star. The name Phosphorus was also attributed to the fallen angel Lucifer.

Love has always been associated with the planet Venus. This is reflected in a peculiarity of Venus, for it is said that *"love makes time stand still"*, and the Venusian day is longer than the Venusian year! It takes Venus 225 days to orbit the Sun, but 243 days to rotate on its axis, giving it the longest day of any planet. Venus also rotates in the opposite direction to the other planets, so from Venus the sun would appear to rise in the West and set in the East.

Love has inspired much of the great art in history, from literature and paintings to sculpture and jewellery. For this reason Venus is known as the inspirer of the arts and creativity.

Love is expressed in different ways, and this is also reflected in the different Venusian qualities like creativity, pleasure, sensuality and sexuality. This is particularly seen in the ancient Greek language, with different words for the different types of love. Thus there is *agapé* (spiritual love), *eros* (physical love), *storge* (familial love) and *philia* (friendship).

Sociability is another Venusian quality, as friendships also usually have a level of attraction of some sort, (even if not sexual), and relationships require communication and an ability to function in social circumstances.

Negative Venusian qualities are associated with attraction, love and sexuality, such as jealousy and lasciviousness. These qualities may all be overcome by working with positive Venusian ones.

# The Moon - Works of Mystery

*"From the Moon, a peacemaking Consonancy, fecundity, the power of Generating & growing greater, of Increasing & Decreasing; A Moderate Temperance & faith, which being Conversant in Manifest & occult things, yieldeth Direction to all, also Motion to the tilling of the Earth, for the manner of Life, & giving growth to it self & others."*[6]

| | |
|---|---|
| **Numbers** | 9, 13, 81, 999 |
| **Colour** | Silver, White |
| **Rules** | Cancer |
| **Metal** | Silver |
| **Day of the Week** | Monday |
| **Element** | Water |
| **Direction** | North-West |
| **Concepts** | Astral Work, Birth, Clairvoyance, Cycles, Divination, Dreams, Glamour, Illusions, Increase & Decrease, Madness, Shapeshifting, Spells, Spirituality, Tides, Transformation, Unconscious |
| **Tools** | Bow & Arrow, Magick Mirror, Perfumes, Sandals |
| **Deities** | Artemis, Bendis, Diana, Hekate, Isis, Khonsu, Luna, Selene, Sin, Thoth |
| **Archangel** | Gabriel |

6 The Keys to the Gateway of Magic.

The Moon is the fifth largest planetary satellite in our solar system, though it is much larger in comparison to the Earth than any of the other moons to their planets. The Moon orbits the Earth every 27.3 days, taking 29.5 days to rotate on its own axis.

Along with the Sun, the Moon is the most visible object in the sky, and the most obviously significant. The Moon has played a role in religions and magick since time immemorial. The changing face of the Moon was the basis of early calendars, providing a way to measure the passing of time in cycles.

The Moon pulls the tides of the oceans, and through this action is intimately connected with water. As the human body is mostly water, it is easy to see why so many people should feel influenced by the Moon. The extreme of this is of course *"full moon madness"*, the source of the term lunatic for people whose behaviour became more erratic at the Full Moon.

The tidal influence of the Moon is also used in magick to describe the effects of the Moon phases. Thus a waxing Moon from new to full is considered to be a time of increase, as the light level grows, and the waning Moon from full to dark is considered a time of decrease, as the light level diminishes.

As the strongest light source during the hours of night, the Moon has come to be connected with the unseen, the unconscious, dreams, and psychic powers. This has resulted in the power of the Moon being greatly emphasised in magickal work, as it is seen as encouraging the development of the psychic senses, and holding sway during the hours when people are normally sleeping, when dreams are expressing the language of the unconscious.

With its cyclic nature, the Moon is associated with events from both the beginning and end of life. Thus both birth and communication with the dead are connected with the Moon.

Negative lunar qualities include delusion, fantasy-prone nature, and inconstancy. Working with positive lunar qualities can overcome all of these.

# Mars - Works of Power

*"From Mars, constant Courage & fortitude, not to be terrified, truth, a fervent Desire of animosity, the power & practice of Acting, and an Inconvertible Vehemency of the mind."*[7]

| | |
|---|---|
| **Numbers** | 5, 25, 125, 555 |
| **Colour** | Red |
| **Rules** | Aries, co-rules Scorpio |
| **Metal** | Iron, Brass |
| **Day of the Week** | Tuesday |
| **Element** | Fire |
| **Direction** | South-West |
| **Concepts** | Anger, Atavism, Conflict, Courage, Ego, Energy, Lycanthropy, Passion, Sex Drive, Strength, Vengeance, Vigour |
| **Tools** | Anvil, Burin, Hammer, Scourge, Spear, Whip |
| **Deities** | Ares, Bellona, Horus, Mars, Nergal |
| **Archangel** | Khamael |

7 The Keys to the Gateway of Magic.

Mars is also known as the *"Red Planet"*, due to its colour when viewed in the night sky. The ancient Greek name for Mars was *Piroesis*, meaning *"the fiery one"*. The Babylonians named Mars after their fiery war god Nergal.

It is the fourth planet from the Sun, and of all the planets Mars is the most like the Earth, having a *"day"* of around 24½ hours, although its diameter is just over half that of the Earth, and its year much longer at 687 days. Mars was originally associated with agriculture, and subsequently became a war god, a reflection of human development from man's early agricultural roots being overtaken by his bellicose nature. Mars has two moons, *Phobos* (*"fear"*) and *Deimos* (*"terror"*), named after the sons of Ares, the Greek war god equated with Mars by the Romans. Both moons are very small and are thought to be captured asteroids.

Mars is associated with sexuality, through its passion, vigour and energy. Because of its connection to wolves and the primitive instinctual nature (the *"flight or fight"* instinct), Mars is also associated with lycanthropy, or transformation into animal form (not just werewolves but other were-creatures as well such as were-tigers and were-leopards). In magick this type of primitive transformational energy is sometimes referred to as atavism, and is sometimes utilised for sigils to power them with a strong energising emotional current.[8]

As the *"warrior"* planet, Mars is associated with the appropriate qualities like courage, strength and virility. Mars provides the courage to act and the energy to see the action through to resolution. It also provides the strength to maintain the ego as the social core of identity. The emphasis here is on maintenance, not inflation, which is one of the problems that can be encountered when the powerful energies of Mars are flowing freely.

The energy of Mars can be turned to constructive or destructive ends. This is well illustrated through its metal, iron, which can be used to make ploughshares or scalpels to nurture and heal, or swords to kill (or guard of

---

8 See in particular the work of the magickal artist Austin Osman Spare

course). It can also be seen in how you use anger. Anger can be focused and used as a transformational quality, not being directed at any person but used instead to motivate, or it can be allowed to take the easy route of aggression and weaken you by making you act in a negative manner.

Mars in its negative state brings abusiveness, arrogance, bullying, destructiveness, disruptiveness, egotism, profanity, self-centredness, stubbornness, violence, and wrath. Such conditions can be countered with positive Martial qualities, and removed from the nature, though stubbornness is by its nature a difficult trait to dispel.

# Jupiter - Works of Expansion

*"From Jupiter an unshaken prudence, temperance, benignity, piety, Modesty, justice, faith, Grace, Religion, Equity & Regality, &c."*[9]

| **Numbers** | 4, 16, 64, 444 |
|---|---|
| **Colour** | Blue, Purple |
| **Rules** | Sagittarius co-rules Pisces |
| **Metal** | Tin |
| **Day of the Week** | Thursday |
| **Element** | Air/Water |
| **Direction** | South-East |
| **Concepts** | Ascendancy, Authority, Body Health, Devotion, Enthusiasm, Ethics, Expansion, Fortune, Honour, Humour, Law, Luck, Morals, Politics, Religion, Responsibility, Rulership, Tyranny, Truth, Wealth |
| **Tools** | Crook, Dorje, Mace, Sceptre |
| **Deities** | Amun, Dolichenus, Fortuna, Jupiter, Marduk, Zeus |
| **Archangel** | Tzadkiel |

9 The Keys to the Gateway of Magic.

Jupiter is the largest of the planets, and the fifth out from the Sun. It has at least sixty-three moons, the largest of these being considerably larger than the Earth's Moon. Unlike other planets, Jupiter radiates more heat than it absorbs from the Sun, hence its connection to expansiveness. Jupiter was the ruler of the gods, and its associated qualities reflect this position.

The ancient Greeks associated Jupiter with Zeus and called it *Phaethon,* meaning *"the bright one"*. In the Middle Ages Jupiter was known as the *"Great Benefic"*, and was seen as one of the most positive and benevolent of planets. It is associated with the establishment, with religion, the power structure, and hence is connected to rulership, and its consequence of politics.

Jupiter is concerned with the ethics and behaviour of the individual, in how they express themselves in society, so the strength of Jupiter in a person can be seen through the level of morality they demonstrate in their behaviour. Because of its association with both ethics and rulership, Jupiter is associated with law. Law is the domain of the ruler, with his sceptre symbolising his ability to dispense power through others without needing to act personally. However with law comes the danger of abuse to those in powerful (Jupiterian) positions, or the old adage of *"one law for the rich and another for the poor"*.

The word jovial comes from Jove, another name for Jupiter. Humour and enthusiasm are both positive Jupiterian qualities. Jupiter is also associated with expansion, and for this reason is connected to success in business and other ventures, particularly when you need to *"gain the upper hand"*.

Bodily health is also associated with Jupiter, the idea of having a strong healthy body to enable you to pursue your goals in life, both material and spiritual, without the hindrance of regular illness.

With its attribution to religion and spirituality, the expression of individual spirituality also reflects the Jupiterian influence in a person. Devotional work is usually associated with Jupiter. Devotion entails the expansion of a relationship with the divine, leading to spiritual expansion and success in walking your path. Truth is the goal of all spiritual seekers, and is also the foundation of ethics and morals, making it one of the most important of Jupiterian concepts.

The negative qualities of Jupiter are bigotry, covetousness, hypocrisy, prejudice, recklessness, self-indulgence and tyranny. Working with the positive qualities of Jupiter can help neutralise these tendencies, all of which can be permanently dispelled from the personality freeing energy for spiritual growth.

# Saturn - Works of Form

*"From Saturn man receiveth a sublime contemplation, profound understanding, solidity of Judgement, firm speculation, stability and an immovable Resolution."*[10]

| | |
|---|---|
| **Numbers** | 3, 9, 29, 333 |
| **Colour** | Black, Brown |
| **Rules** | Capricorn, co-rules Aquarius |
| **Metal** | Lead |
| **Day of the Week** | Saturday |
| **Element** | Earth |
| **Direction** | North |
| **Concepts** | Agriculture, Austerity, Duty, Equilibrium, Formation, History, Legal Matters, Limitation, Patience, Practicality, Prudence, Restriction, Self-Discipline, Teaching, Time, Wisdom |
| **Tools** | Hourglass, Scythe, Scales, Shadows, Sickle, Veil |
| **Deities** | Janus, Kronos, Ninib, Saturn |
| **Archangel** | Tzaphkiel |

10 The Keys to the Gateway of Magic.

Saturn is the second largest of the planets, and is the sixth out from the Sun. Saturn is best known for its spectacular rings, which are mainly ice particles combined with particles of dust thought to be the remains of moons which were destroyed in the past. Saturn has fifty-six moons (at last count!), mostly named after characters from Greek and Roman myths.

The largest moon of Saturn is called Titan, and it is the only moon in our universe dense enough to have an atmosphere. Many of the other moons are named after actual Titans from the Greek myths. To the ancient Greeks Saturn was known as *Phainon,* meaning *"the shiny one"*, and associated with the god Kronos.

Saturn takes just under 29½ years to orbit the Sun, this period of time being known in Astrology as the Saturn Return. The Saturn Return is when the planet returns to the same place in the heavens as it was when you were born, and is thought to usually herald major life changes.

Saturn is the most maligned of the planets, as can be seen from its old name of the *"Great Malefic"*. This is very unfair when we remember that the Roman god Saturn was the ruler of the Golden Age, and was the god who taught man agriculture and how to sow seeds. Saturn is associated with time and form, the solidity of matter.

In ancient times Saturn was the most distant planet visible to man, and so set the boundaries of the universe. As the outer boundary it is easy to see why Saturn should be associated with time and boundaries.

Saturn is a great teacher. In the energy of Saturn you learn balance and self-discipline, how to deal with the material world. Though structures and laws may sometimes seem restrictive, they provide the physical framework you need to function, and remind you of your duty in a social and personal situation. Only when you understand how things work and are competent in performing them can you effectively move on beyond the limits of the current situation. The patience, prudence and practicality of Saturn are all vital qualities for maintaining a healthy balance in your life and not being overwhelmed by excessive tides of emotion or energy.

In Qabalah, Saturn is attributed to the Sephira of Binah, and is associated with the feminine divine as the Dark Mother. Binah is also known as the City of Pyramids, a good analogy to the power of Saturn, as the apex can be seen as the place where force manifests down into the form of the pyramid. As the only planet with a density less than water, the associated quality of being the transitional place between force and form is particularly appropriate for Saturn.

The negative qualities of Saturn are anguish, desperation, lying, madness, melancholy, obstinacy, rigidity, sadness, and tedium. All of these states can be countered by working with the positive qualities of the planet. Some of these qualities can be permanently removed, but others like melancholy and sadness can creep back in and must be countered whenever they occur.

CHAPTER 3

# The Planetary Deities

The deities associated with the seven classical planets have remained fairly constant for more than two thousand years. They take their names from the old Roman gods: Sol, Mercury, Venus, Luna, Mars, Jupiter and Saturn. Most of these Roman planetary gods can be seen as part of an extended family, which also includes the deities associated with the trans-Saturnian planets. This can be seen in the family tree:

- ⊕ Uranus is the father of Saturn, and Venus
- ⊕ Saturn is the father of Jupiter, Neptune and Pluto
- ⊕ Jupiter is the father of Mercury and Mars

It is interesting and significant that the two luminaries of the Sun and Moon, Sol and Luna, were brother and sister, and come from a different line, which equated to the Greek Titans Hyperion and Theia. This separation of the seven classical planets into the five *"real"* planets and the two luminaries (Sun and Moon) is repeatedly emphasised in planetary attributions.

The Romans equated their own deities to those of the earlier Greek culture during the period of expansion of the Roman Empire, in doing so they absorbed many of the qualities and myths of the Greek deities into those of their own. As a result of this conflation it would be more accurate to say that the planetary gods may be considered to be Romano-Greek in nature.

The idea of attributing deities to the seven classical planets did not however originate with the Romans or indeed the Greeks. When considering the history of these attributions we find that it is one which was also practiced by the much earlier Babylonians and that this may indeed have provided the inspiration for the Greeks to name the planets after their own gods. When the Greeks conquered the ancient Babylonians they considered the qualities associated with the Babylonian deities and through comparison with that of their own, named the planets after the deities in their own pantheon with corresponding qualities. Thus if we follow the sequence of attribution to the planets through these cultures from Babylonian to Greek to Roman, we see:

| Planet | Babylonian | Greek | Roman | Common Qualities |
|---|---|---|---|---|
| Sun | Shamash | Helios | Sol | Solar Gods |
| Mercury | Nabu | Hermes | Mercury | Messengers of the Gods |
| Venus | Ishtar | Aphrodite | Venus | Goddesses of Love |
| Moon | Sin | Selene | Luna | Lunar Deities |
| Mars | Nergal | Ares | Mars | War Gods |
| Jupiter | Marduk | Zeus | Jupiter | Father Gods, Bringers of Order |
| Saturn | Ninib | Kronos | Saturn | Planters of Seeds |

The benefits of working with the planetary deities can be summarised by two possibilities, either receiving energy from the deity or striving towards a greater purity and power as expressed by the deity. Both these approaches can be seen most clearly in ancient Greek writings. The former attitude of requesting divine aid is seen throughout writings seeking to achieve magickal results, particularly the *Greek Magickal Papyri.* It is also seen in writings such as the *Homeric Hymns,* where offerings are made to the deity being hymned in an attempt to encourage a gift of divine energy.

The second reason is particularly well expressed by the Neoplatonic philosopher Iamblichus (c.245-325 CE) in his Theurgic writings. He preached the journey of the soul to perfection through union with the perfected power of the deities, through the development of facets of the self by identification with the different deities. Thus Iamblichus wrote of hymns that they:

*"Do not draw down the impassive and pure Gods to that which is passive and impure, but on the contrary, it renders us … pure and immutable."*[11]

11 On the Mysteries of the Egyptians, Chaldeans, and Assyrians, I.12.

# The Solar God

Sol, meaning *"Sun"*, was a major Roman God. He was also known as Sol Invictus (*"invincible Sun"*), a title shared at times by the Persian warrior god Mithras. As well as Mithras, he was also equated at times with the Greek solar gods Apollo and Helios, and the Egyptian solar god Ra and Sumerian solar god Shamash. Sol was the brother of the goddesses Luna and Aurora.

The Sun God is the lord of light, the eternal illuminating fire, all-seeing and hence all-knowing. His radiant generative power makes him a ruler god in many pantheons, orbited by the other deities like the planets orbit the Sun. He is apotropaic in nature, driving away evil by shining his stellar light into the darkest recesses. This is why the Athenians of ancient Greece called him *Alexicacon*, or *"averter of evil"*. His rays of light are often equated to golden arrows, and he is hence known as *Arcitenens* (*"bow shooter"*), and Apollo with his bow and arrows, and the arrows of the ferocious Egyptian goddess

Sekhmet illustrate this principle. The radiance of the Sun God emphasises his beauty, the pure and honest virtue of the wise governor of the daylight hours, unconquerable and enduring.

Sol is shown as a man seated or standing in a golden chariot drawn by two lions or four golden horses, sometimes winged. He may be depicted with solar rays emanating from his head or a radiant solar disk face, and he bears a sceptre of power in his right hand. He may also be depicted with a whip in one hand, or with a golden bow and arrows.

## Hymn to Sol

Hear me golden lord whose eternal eye
Sees all as it illuminates the sky
Lord of the seasons with your fiery crown
Self-born fierce god of mighty renown
Agile and vigorous thou venerable Sun
In bright splendour around the heavens you run
Source of existence pure and fiery bright
All-knowing all-pervading light
Blessed with immortal flames to set and rise
Revealing all that occurs beneath your awesome eyes
O Sol the faithful defender and eye of might
You shine with life and power and light
Propitious on my labours shine
And bless me with thy rays divine

# The Mercurial God

Mercury is the Roman god of communication, magick and merchants, whose name may come from the root *"merx"* meaning *"merchandise"*. Mercury was the son of Jupiter and the nymph Maia. He was a precocious child, inventing the lyre when he was a few days old. He was a great joker and mischief and theft are also qualities associated with him. He was equated to the Greek God Hermes, who had similar characteristics, the Egyptian magick god Thoth, the Thracian god Zalmoxis and the Sumerian messenger god Nebu.

As the god of the mind, Mercury is the great inventor, the bringer of inspiration and also the healer. He was said to have invented writing after watching the shape cranes make when they fly, and given it to men, whence he was known as *Ermeneutes,* meaning *"interpreter"*. He was also the god of diplomacy and social interaction. Mercury is a god of journeying, the psychopomp who travels between the worlds, and is thus a god of the liminal, often to be found guarding gateways or mediating disputes. Another important attribute of Mercury is that he is the god of astronomy and astrology, and he also invented the calendar, ordering the months. Mercury was the god of dogs, which were seen as his sacred animal.

Mercury was commonly depicted as a beautiful young man, with winged sandals and a winged helmet indicating his role as the messenger of the Gods, often bearing the caduceus and/or a money bag, and occasionally a golden winged cape. He was also sometimes depicted as a mature bearded man.

## Hymn to Mercury

Mercury draw near and to my words incline
Master of magick and psychopomp divine
Celestial messenger of awesome skill
Whose skills and humour does all mortals thrill
Bestower of sacred wisdom in thy speech
Quicksilver speed beyond all human reach
With heart almighty and a cunning mind
You gave the gift of healing to mankind
O liminal traveller to rejoice is thine
In art and craft and music all sublime
Sharper than a sword thy tongue which men revere
Hear my words great Mercury and draw near
Assist my work and bless me with your peace
A grace in speech and memory's increase

# The Venusian Goddess

Venus is the Roman goddess of love and gardens, who became associated with the Greek love goddess Aphrodite. Her name may mean *"love"*, *"beauty"* or *"sexual desire"*. She was also equated to the Sumerian goddess Ishtar, the Egyptian cow goddess Hathor and the Assyrian goddess Astarte. There are two different birth myths for Venus, either she was born from the genitals of Uranus which had been thrown into the sea, or she was the daughter of Jupiter with the goddess Dione. Venus was known by many titles, including Amica (*"Friend"*), Aurea (*"Golden"*), Caelestis (*"Celestial"*), Felix (*"Lucky"*), and Genetrix (*"Mother"*). She was sometimes also portrayed with a helmet and/or shield as Venus Victrix (*"Victorious"*).

She is the goddess of all the qualities associated with love, such as beauty, desire, grace and pleasure, and also love poetry and songs. Venus is also a goddess of procreation, in humans and animals, the natural result of sex. Her girdle of love and desire was irresistible and represented the cosmic power of attraction, which constantly acted in balance with the power or repulsion (or strife). Only three deities were immune to her girdle, the goddesses Diana, Minerva and Vesta (or their Greek equivalents of Artemis, Athena and Hestia).

Venus is shown as a beautiful naked woman, sometimes bearing a flaming heart in her right hand. She is sometimes depicted accompanied by birds or by Eros, as a winged cherub bearing bow and arrow. Birds were particularly associated with her, and she was occasionally depicted riding side-saddle on a goose or swan, or in a chariot drawn by doves. When travelling across seas she would ride in a cockle shell chariot pulled by tritons.

## Hymn to Venus

Beautiful heavenly laughter-loving queen
Your radiance always the first and last to be seen
Source of persuasion secret favouring queen
Illustrious born apparent and unseen
Desiring, most desired, harsh and kind
To thee are men and women all inclined
With magick chains you bind through love's fair grace
To chance a single glance of your heavenly face
The strongest power in your girdle rests
That frees us through the fires of your tests
Choirs of nymphs sing praises to your name
Not even gods can ever hope your heart to tame
Come most beautiful to my prayer inclined
To thee I call with holy love and praise in mind

# The Lunar Goddess

Luna is the Roman name for the Moon. Like her brother Helios, Luna was a child of the Titans Theia ("*Sight*") and Hyperion ("*the One above*"), along with her sister Aurora ("*the Dawn*"). This goddess was sometimes equated to other goddesses from the Roman and Greek pantheons, such as Diana, Artemis, Selene and Hekate, as well as the Thracian goddess Bendis. She was worshipped from early Roman times in her own right, but less has been recorded about her due to her conflation with other lunar goddesses.

Luna is a goddess of birth, and of the growth of plants and animals. She is the illuminating light in the darkness of night, reflecting the tides she pulls in her ever-changing face. In this context she was seen as a protectress for travellers on earth and sea by night. She was also regarded as a dispenser of fate, a nurturing goddess who nourished mankind through her benevolence.

Luna is shown as a beautiful naked or semi-naked woman standing on a crescent, bearing a torch in her left hand. She may also be winged, have a lunar crescent on her brow and stars above her head. Luna was sometimes depicted riding a stag or bull, or in a silver chariot pulled by two or four winged horses, or by a team of oxen.

## Hymn to Luna

Hear me, gracious goddess, diffusing your silvery light
As horned and radiant you travel through the night
Surrounded by stars in your orbit wide
Your torch extended through the heavens you ride
Reflecting borrowed solar rays you shine
Now growing to full, now tending to decline
Mother of ages, thou fruit-producing queen
Lover of life your touch on the waters is seen
Fair lady of night, illuminator and friend
You give to nature's works their destined end
Clad in a shimmering robe and shining veil
Queen of the night to thee Luna I hail
Shine on my sacred rite with your prosperous rays
And receive from me my deep and ardent praise

# The Martial God

Mars is the tutelary god of the Romans, the son of Jupiter and Juno. He was worshipped as a war god, but was originally an agriculture god. His name may be derived from the Etruscan agriculture god Maris. The wolf was particularly associated with Mars as his sacred animal, and this is particularly seen in the story of the founding of Rome, with the she-wolf that suckled Romulus and Remus. The month of March is named after him and he was given a whole range of titles, which were appended to his name and reflected his qualities. These included Augustus (*"Imperial"*), Conservator (*"the Preserver"*), Militarus (*"Military"*), Pacifer (*"the Peacemaker"*), Pater (*"Father"*), Ultor (*"the Avenger"*), and Victor (*"the Victorious"*).

Mars is a god of qualities associated with war and conflict, such as anger, courage, strength, bloodshed, violence, cowardice, fear and terror. He was seen as both the defender and sacker of cities.

Mars is shown as a strong warrior, helmeted and either naked or in Roman-style armour with a short leather tunic underneath, bearing a sword in his right hand and shield in his left. He is sometimes depicted on or in front of a lion, or in a chariot pulled by lions or fiery horses.

## Hymn to Mars

Mighty unconquered fiery Mars
In strength rejoicing amongst the stars
Fierce and untamed your mighty power can make
Even the strongest walls to their foundations shake
Evil destroying king covered with gore
Dispelling the demons with your dreadful roar
In blood and sword and spears you delight
Always ready to win the fight
Your power in the fields is also great
To strengthen the crops and harvests you create
You lend your force to honourable men
Your strategies victorious again and again
Encourage my work to valour inclined
And give success with benevolent mind

# The Jupiterian God

Jupiter is the king of the gods of the Roman pantheon, the sky god who bore the celestial thunder and lightning. He is the first deity of the Capitoline triad (with the goddesses Juno and Minerva), and his name means *"Father God"*. As such an important and popular deity it is not surprising that the Romans equated other major deities with him, including the Greek Zeus, Egyptian Amun and the Syrian Dolichenus. His sacred animals were the eagle and the bull.

Jupiter is the god of the weather, fate, and law and order. He is the most prolific shape-shifter of the planetary gods, taking on a whole range of animal forms to seduce mortal women and nymphs, often producing semi-divine children. He is the Father God of the pantheon, and he lived up to this role with his huge number of children. Jupiter was also known as Jove, which is the root for the word jovial, and humour was associated with Jupiter. His

Greek counterpart Zeus was the god of games, with the Olympic Games being held in his honour.

Jupiter was depicted as a kingly bearded man in his prime often shown bearing his thunderbolts or a sceptre or lance, and sometimes a patera (offering plate). He is sometimes depicted riding an eagle, griffin or a winged stag. The oak tree was sacred to him, and he was occasionally represented wearing a wreath of oak leaves.

## Hymn to Jupiter

O greatly honoured Jupiter supremely great
To thee this rite I dedicate
My prayers and exaltations to thee king divine
For all things round thy head exalted shine
Magnanimous commanding sceptred god
Even nature trembles at your mighty nod
Loud-sounding armed with bolts of thunder
With lightning flash the sky you sunder
Source of abundance and purifying king
Many-formed from whom mercies spring
Benevolent laughter roaring through the sky
I call to you enthroned in the heavens on high
Propitious hear my prayer and give good health
With peace divine and necessary wealth

# The Saturnian God

Saturn is the Roman god who ruled the Golden Age of Mankind when all life was in harmony, and ruled over seed sowing, as seen by the meaning of his name as *"Sower"*. Saturn was the son of Uranus, whose rule he overthrew, and the father of Jupiter, who subsequently copied his father's deed and overthrew him. He was equated to the Greek Kronos, the associated myths then being transferred to him.

Saturn is the god of time, known for his wisdom and intelligence. He had the ability to raise or depress the thoughts of men, and for this reason is associated with preservation and destruction, inspiration and melancholy. He was also known by the title of Coelius (*"Heavenly"*). After his deposal he became the ruler of the Isles of the Blessed, a paradisiacal afterlife realm. During the Golden Age of Saturn honey was said to flow from trees, and honey was sacred to him.

Saturn is depicted as an old but strong bearded man, wearing a crown and bearing a scythe. He is sometimes shown riding a crowned winged dragon, and occasionally bearing an hour-glass.

## Hymn to Saturn

My words, mighty Saturn do hear
Father of Gods, whom all revere
Bless me with your wisdom pure and strong
To you perfection and decrease belong
You consume all that has reached its time to die
And replace it with the new growth you supply
Father of eternity, vast and divine
The blossoms of earth and the stars are thine
From your seeds do various forms of being shoot
The bud, the branch, the blossom and the root
O lord of form, of time, of subtle mind
Towards my words may your gracious powers be inclined

CHAPTER 4

# Meditation Journeys

A meditation journey is exactly as the name suggests, a mental journey you undertake in a meditative state to explore your inner landscape. The purpose of such journeys is to integrate aspects of your psyche during the journey, to becoming as perfect as you can be. From this perspective it can be seen that meditation journeys involving encounters with deities are actually a form of theurgy, the quest to perfect the soul by identification with the qualities of the gods.

For this reason we recommend that a hymn to the planetary deity should be performed before undertaking the meditation journey. This will act as an invitation to the deity without, to express itself as a facet of the divine spark of the soul within, so that through this interaction the soul is brought closer to perfection.

Meditation journeys are a simple yet effective tool, which can be performed with as little or as much ceremony as you desire. By placing the journey within a ceremonial context you give greater emphasis to the inner transformations you seek to effect. The setting for the meditation journey should be a quiet space. They can be performed in a quiet room or at night out under the stars if you have access to a safe and quiet outdoor space away from light pollution. The use of incense and a subtle magick circle prior to a meditation journey both add to the clarity of the journey by enhancing your mood and focusing your mind on the task at hand.

It is recommended that you make a recording of the meditation journey to play during your ceremony. If you read the journey, you obviously cannot be in a meditative state. You can memorise the journey and follow it, but again your concentration is then of necessity not on getting the full benefits of the details your mind supplies. These details should be noted afterwards whenever possible, as they are indicators of the symbolic language of your unconscious. By recording additional detail in this manner over a period of time, you are creating a symbolic dictionary for your own unconscious, which you can use over time to gain greater understanding of visionary images and dreams.

As with other types of meditation, these journeys should be performed sitting or seated, not lying down. Whether you are sitting or seated for meditation, it is always preferable to sit with your spine straight. Never slouch when you are meditating, as the bad posture inhibits internal energy flow. Begin each journey by taking a few deep breaths, allowing your body and mind to relax and in so doing, prepare yourself for the journey you will be undertaking.

The journeys that follow can be used for both solitary and group use. Each in turn introduces the participant(s) to the deity associated with one of the seven wandering stars and allows for exploration of the symbolism, ideas and mythologies associated with each in turn. They can be used as introductory workings, which can be expanded upon in due course as they provide clear symbolic images of the deities which are useful as a core around which to create further journeys exploring the deeper mysteries of each planet.

# Journey to the God Sol

Sit comfortably and relax, closing your eyes. In your mind's eye fix the image of yourself sitting as you are in the room. Hold this image, and then see a white mist filling the room, obscuring the walls, the floor, the ceiling, everything, until all around you is white mist.

The white mist disperses and you find yourself looking down at the earth from a great height. Taking stock of your surroundings you realise you are in a golden chariot pulled by four golden winged horses, flying through the heavens. Standing next to you is a beautiful man dressed in golden armour with a golden helmet, with light radiating from him. You realise he is Sol, the sun god.

As you fly through the heavens, you notice for all the horses' movement the chariot hardly seems to move in the sky. You look down at the earth below, enjoying the incredible perspective, with the earth beneath you. Everything is clearly illuminated by the sunlight shining down upon it.

You see a brilliant light, and watch as a flaming bird rises to the sky and flies past. The phoenix leaves a trail of golden sparks in its wake. Even light and fire must be periodically renewed, it seems to say, as a single flaming feather drifts into the chariot and lands at your feet.

Sol speaks to you and says, *"When you live your entire life in the light, you welcome the brief kiss of an eclipse. With my sister I am one side of the cycle. Though I live eternally in my own light, it is too bright for you to live in. Though my light brings life, it also burns in extremes. Even though you may seek the light, you must also learn from the darkness, which has its own power."*

You know that light and dark, night and day, are balanced, and wonder at his words. You think about how balanced the forces are in your life. However you also realise that the solar light of illumination is necessary to guide your way and bring the life-giving energy of the Sun into your life.

You look down again at the feather, which is still burning, and as you look you see the white mist forming and surrounding you until once again all around you is white mist. Again the mist disperses, and as it fades away you find yourself once more sitting in the room.

Take some time to write up your experience and contemplate what you have learned.

# Journey to the God Mercury

Sit comfortably and relax, closing your eyes. In your mind's eye fix the image of yourself sitting as you are in the room. Hold this image, and then see a white mist filling the room, obscuring the walls, the floor, the ceiling, everything, until all around you is white mist. As the mist disperses you find yourself in an underground tunnel made of grey granite, with torches on the walls alternately every 5m. About 20m ahead there is a doorway into a vault.

Entering the vault, you see it is about 20m square and has roughly hewn walls. The ceiling is 3m above you, and in the centre of the vault is a beautiful young man sitting on a golden throne, he has a grin on his face and his eyes are full of laughter. He wears a simple white tunic and has a winged helmet on his head and winged sandals on his feet. In his right hand he holds a caduceus.

The throne he sits on is flanked by two pillars each 1m in diameter, rising from the floor to the ceiling. The pillar on the left of the throne is made of gold, and the one on the right is made of a single piece of emerald. Approaching the throne you see that there is a golden casket sitting on the floor in front of Mercury. The casket is 30cm by 20cm by 10cm deep. Mercury asks you how much the truth matters to you? He tells you he is the master of guile, but even lies work best when interwoven with the truth, like the two serpents of his caduceus. However, he insists, truth must be your guiding light on your path and you should never lie to yourself.

He touches the end of the caduceus to the casket, and you hear the lock click. Look inside, he tells you, so you lift the lid, struggling slightly with the weight, and open it. Within the casket is a single tablet of emerald, filling the casket. On the emerald tablet there are strange hieroglyphs. As you look at the hieroglyphs they seem to shift in front of your eyes. The first line says *"With certainty, that which is above is as that which is below"*. As you continue to stare at the tablet, the words speak to you, and you realise that the truth on the emerald tablet is an ever-changing message that varies with the observer.

Remember as fully as you can the words you read on the emerald tablet so you can consider them and meditate on them afterwards.

Mercury laughs and you lift your gaze from the emerald tablet to see him looking at you from the throne. He has changed and his face is now that of a bearded mature man. His transformation reminds you that everything changes and that people can wear many faces. Nodding to you, he vanishes and the white mist appears, filling the vault around you, until once again you are surrounded by white mist. Again the mist disperses, and as it fades away you find yourself once more sitting in the room.

Take some time to write up your experience and contemplate what you have learned.

# Journey to the Goddess Venus

Sit comfortably and relax, closing your eyes. In your mind's eye fix the image of yourself sitting as you are in the room. Hold this image, and then see a white mist filling the room, obscuring the walls, the floor, the ceiling, everything, until all around you is white mist. As the mist disperses you find yourself at the bottom of a mound with a temple on it.

The temple is a heptagon about 10m across, set at the top of seven marble steps which lead up to it. There are seven marble pillars of classic design placed equidistantly around the top of the base at the points of the heptagon rising 3m into the air. On top of the pillars there are marble lintels all the way around them. Growing up the pillars are rose vines, with roses of a different rainbow colour around each pillar. Sitting on top of the pillars are doves, cooing happily.

Climbing the steps and passing between two pillars you see a marble fountain in the centre of the temple, with water shooting up about 1m in the air. The scent of roses fills the air around you, and looking up you see that there is no roof, you can see the sun in the clear blue sky above you. At the base of the fountain is a hand-mirror, set in a copper frame. As you look at the mirror you see a flaming heart inside it.

You reach to pick up the mirror but as you do so a beautifully formed female hand beats you to it and picks the mirror up. As your gaze lifts to see the woman who has picked up the mirror, you see the most beautiful woman you have ever seen, and realise that this is the goddess Venus. Her simple white tunic cannot conceal the perfection of her form underneath it, and the radiance of her face takes your breath away.

Venus smiles at you and your heart almost stops. She says *"Love comes in many forms,"* and offers you the mirror. Thanking her you take the mirror, and ay you look into it you realise it does not show your reflection, but that of your first love. As you continue to look at it, the image changes and a sequence of all the people you have loved is shown through the reflection, lovers, family, close friends. If you are looking for love, offer a prayer to Venus to show you the face of your love-to-be, and wait for a face to appear in the reflection.

When you have finished looking in the mirror you return it to Venus with your thanks, and she points to the waters of the fountain, suggesting you take a drink of the waters of love if you wish to bring more love into your life or ease the pain of love lost. You thank her once more and kneel by the fountain to cup your hands into the water. Lowering your head to drink the water you have cupped up, its cool refreshing taste reminds you of strawberries.

As you look up you see that Venus has disappeared, and the white mist is rolling in, obscuring the fountain, the temple, the sky, everything around you, until once again you are surrounded by white mist. Again the mist disperses, and as it fades away you find yourself once more sitting in the room.

Take some time to write up your experience and contemplate what you have learned.

# Journey to the Goddess Luna

Sit comfortably and relax, closing your eyes. In your mind's eye fix the image of yourself sitting as you are in the room. Hold this image, and then see a white mist filling the room, obscuring the walls, the floor, the ceiling, everything, until all around you is white mist. As the mist disperses you find yourself in a silver chariot pulled through the night sky by four silver horses.

Standing next to you in the chariot is a beautiful woman with long silver hair in a flowing silver dress. As silver light radiates from her you know this is Luna, the moon goddess, travelling her course through the night. Her light dims a little, and as you look forward you see one of the front horses turns black.

You keep looking around, at the stars above, and the dimly lit landscape below, and as you do so her light dims again, and the other front horse turns black. You realise the phases of the moon are reflected through her light and the colour of her horses.

*"Understanding the nature of cycles will help you move forward on your path,"* Luna tells you, *"the ebbs and flows of your own nature and how they respond to your environment."* As she speaks her light dims further, and you know a third horse has turned black. She smiles, and her light fades completely, enabling you to look at her beauty easily. You glance forward and see the chariot is now pulled by four black horses.

Though it is darker now, it is easier for you to see the ground below and the stars above. You realise that the dreamlike quality of this journey is a reflection of the power of the moon, and see a silver light emanating from Luna again, and one of the horses turn silver.

*"One of the greatest gifts I give is intuition, always trust yours, for it is there when you have nothing else,"* Luna informs you.

You thank her and watch enraptured as she becomes brighter and brighter again, regaining her former radiance. As she does so all the horses turn silver one by one.

You know this is an endless cycle, and as you watch her, the white mist appears, filling the chariot around you, until once again you are surrounded by white mist. Again the mist disperses, and as it fades away you find yourself once more sitting in your room.

Take some time to write up your experience and contemplate what you have learned.

# Journey to the God Mars

Sit comfortably and relax, closing your eyes. In your mind's eye fix the image of yourself sitting as you are in the room. Hold this image, and then see a white mist filling the room, obscuring the walls, the floor, the ceiling, everything, until all around you is white mist.

The white mist disperses and you find yourself standing in a grove, in front of a large old oak tree. In your hands you are holding a sword and a round shield. As you look up at the branches of the oak tree you see mistletoe growing on the upper branches.

A rustling in the undergrowth alerts you to the presence of other life and you turn around so your back is to the tree. Stepping from the trees is the tall figure of a warrior bearing an axe. You bang your sword against your shield to draw his attention and he stares pointedly at you. He demands you step out of the way so he can cut the oak tree down. You refuse and explain that the oak is ancient, a sacred tree that supports all sorts of life and is central to the grove it is in. Listening to you, the warrior first shakes his head, and then slowly starts nodding in agreement. When you have finished explaining he takes his axe and walks away back into the woods.

Almost immediately another figure steps from the trees, again carrying a large axe. He also demands you step aside to let him cut down the oak. You refuse and start to explain about the oak, but he ignores your words and runs at you waving his axe. You raise your shield in time and deflect his blow, sending him flying. With an angry grunt he rises and charges again. This time you are more ready and parry his blow, knocking him to the ground again with your shield. You warn him that next time you will draw blood.

The warrior pauses and sizes you up. Realising you are serious, he gives you a nod of respect and walks away. More rustling warns you that another person is coming. As you wait, you see a large attractive and powerful man in a breastplate bearing a sword and shield walking towards you. He stops and hails you, and you realise this is Mars.

He speaks to you and says: "*You have shown your willingness to fight when you need to, and as a warrior not do more than you need to. Do you always choose your fights as well, and choose your ground appropriately? You should usually be able to win any fight with your mind, and without shaming your opponent. Remember this and the warrior path will always provide you with strength and courage to carry on your way. Hail warrior!*"

With this cry, Mars disappears, leaving you considering his words.

As you look around you see the white mist rising until once again all around you is white mist. Again the mist disperses, and as it fades away you find yourself once more sitting in the room.

Take some time to write up your experience and contemplate what you have learned

# Journey to the God Jupiter

Sit comfortably and relax, closing your eyes. In your mind's eye fix the image of yourself sitting as you are in the room. Hold this image, and then see a white mist filling the room, obscuring the walls, the floor, the ceiling, everything, until all around you is white mist.

The white mist disperses and you find yourself standing on a mountain top, the sun shining down on your brightly from a cloud sky. As you take in the panoramic view of the landscape below you, you can see there has been a storm by the rainbow in the sky, and you feel the freshness in the air around you that a storm always leaves behind.

You see a powerful mature man striding through the air towards you. He wears a blue tunic over his muscular body, and has a golden crown on his head. In his right hand he holds a bunch of thunderbolts. He laughs with a deep roar like thunder as he approaches you, and you know you are in the presence of Jupiter

Jupiter steps on the mountain top next to you, towering over you. Silent he looks over the landscape, and you gain a sense of his rulership of the land below. Not ownership, but rather a stewardship to protect its creatures. As you feel his controlled power emanating from him, you begin to appreciate the qualities needed for a good ruler. The strength tempered with compassion, firmness tempered with humour, justice tempered with mercy. Somehow the role of ruler suddenly seems much more complicated.

Jupiter points to a forest and speaks. *"When left alone the earth always finds her own balance. It is man who throws the balance out. But to influence your environment in a positive way, you must first be the ruler of yourself. Do you rule your own passions, your own fears, your own drives, or do they rule you?"* His piercing gaze holds you fast and you know he sees the truth of your thoughts.

He tells you to hold one of his thunderbolts, and hands it to you. As you take the thunderbolt, there is a huge bang and you find yourself lying on your back on the ground. *"I have taken the first barrier for you, it is up to you to deal with the rest,"* Jupiter says, and strides off into the air, laughing again.

Calling your thanks after him, you ponder his words and what he made you see about yourself, you gaze around, and see the white mist rising until once again all around you is white mist. Again the mist disperses, and as it fades away you find yourself once more sitting in the room.

Take some time to write up your experience and contemplate what you have learned

# Journey to the God Saturn

Sit comfortably and relax, closing your eyes. In your mind's eye fix the image of yourself sitting as you are in the room. Hold this image, and then see a white mist filling the room, obscuring the walls, the floor, the ceiling, everything, until all around you is white mist.

The white mist disperses and you find yourself standing in a field full of golden corn, ripening under the harvest sun. As you look around, you see the fields go on in all directions to the horizon, apart from to your left, where a gentle hill stands out from the corn. On top of the hill you can make out a large throne carved from a single piece of black basalt.

You walk up the hill to look more closely at the throne, and as you approach it you notice an hour-glass carved into the head of the throne. As you admire the workmanship of the throne, a figure walks around from behind the back. It is an old bearded man in a black robe, bearing a scythe, and you realise this is Saturn. Though he is old, there is no sign of weakness or decrepitude in his strong, lithe form. With a nod to you he sits on the throne.

Saturn holds the scythe in his right hand, and you understand that the primary function of the scythe is to reap the harvests he gathers. With this the scythe no longer seems as fearsome. Saturn smiles and the scythe turns into a crow and flies away into the sky. He holds out his left hand, and a black obsidian sphere appears in it. Saturn asks if you would like to take the measure of your life and see where your boundaries end. You thank him and gaze deeply into the obsidian ball.

As you look into the ball, your focus moves entirely onto the images you see within it. You see scenes from your life, of the moments that have defined your path and the person you are. You see your successes and failures, good deeds and mistakes. Through all these visions you realise that there was always the potential for greater success and also greater failure. The boundaries and barriers you have built around yourself become clearer, and you see which of these help you, and which hinder you and hold you back.

The form of your life becomes clearer, and you intuit that the force within your life is your own will, your determination. How much you transform that form by wisely directing your own force is up to you. With this knowledge, you bring your awareness away from the obsidian ball, and in that moment you see that Saturn has disappeared, and in his place an hour-glass sits on the throne.

Gazing at the hour-glass, you observe that it is not sand pouring from the top bulb to the bottom, but seeds. You realise that Saturn is telling you to choose which seeds you plant in your life to harvest later, and not to waste your time being delayed and put off by self-imposed restrictions.

With a smile, you call a thank you to Saturn, and as you do so the white mist rolls in over the fields, obscuring the corn, the sky, the throne, everything, until once again all around you is white mist. Again the mist disperses, and as it fades away you find yourself once more sitting in the room.

Take some time to write up your experience and contemplate what you have learned.

CHAPTER 5

# Planetary Days & Hours

Timing is an important consideration when performing work with the seven classical planets and choosing a favourable time to perform your ceremony is a key factor in securing effective results for your magick.

In order to decide which planetary day or hours to perform your magick in you need to consider the nature of the results you require, so that you will be able to select the most auspicious day and time at which to perform it. Each of the days of the week are associated with one of the classical planets and for this reason it is preferable to perform your ceremony on the day associated with the planetary energy most relevant to your ceremony. When invoking a planetary spirit you would do so on the day of the planet it is associated with, or if you were consecrating a talisman or amulet you would use the day of the week corresponding to the energy you wish to charge it with.

Whichever planet you are working with, in addition to performing your ceremony on the day of the week associated with that planet, it is preferable to also use one of the hours on that day (or night) associated with the planet. If you need to perform a ceremony urgently and it is not practical to wait for the planetary day, you can still use the planetary hours of the planet on any day of the week to tune in to the energies of that planet.

Likewise if a ceremony is for an intent which falls under the influence of two planets, their influence can be combined by using the planetary hour of one of the planets on the planetary day of the other planet. E.g., if you were performing a ceremony for career success, you would notice that this is something which benefits from the influence of both Jupiter and the Sun. Therefore you could tap into the energy of both these planets by either performing your ceremony during a solar hour on a Thursday, or a Jupiterian hour on a Sunday.

| Planet | Types of magick performed on days and in hours |
|---|---|
| Sun | Career success, establishing harmony, healing, improving general health, developing leadership skills, acquiring money, gaining promotion, strengthening willpower |
| Mercury | Business success, improving communication skills and knowledge and memory, diplomacy, succeeding in exams, divining the future, developing influence, protection when travelling by air and land, learning music |
| Venus | Increasing attractiveness and beauty and passion, enhancing creativity, improving fertility, developing friendships, obtaining love, increasing self-confidence |
| Moon | Enhancing clairvoyance, Ensuring safe childbirth, divining the future, developing glamour and illusions, protection when travelling by sea |
| Mars | Controlling anger, increasing courage and energy and passion, increasing sex drive and vigour |
| Jupiter | Career success, developing ambition and enthusiasm, improving fortune and general health, acquiring honour, improving humour, dealing with legal matters and the establishment, developing leadership skills, improving luck |
| Saturn | Performing duty, establishing balance and equilibrium, studying for exams, dispelling illusions, protecting the home, dealing with legal matters, developing patience and self-discipline |

# Planetary Days

The popular sequence of planetary attributions of the days comes from ancient Mesopotamia. This was subsequently adopted by the Greeks, who attributed their deities to the days in accordance with similarities between the qualities and attributes of their deities with the earlier Mesopotamian ones. The Romans then followed the same procedure, replacing the Greek deities with their Roman equivalents. Thus it was that the familiar sequence of Sun, Moon, Mars, Mercury, Jupiter, Venus, and Saturn for the days was established with the Roman deities, i.e. Sunday, Monday, Tuesday, Wednesday, Thursday, Friday, and Saturday.

The association of the planets with the days of the week has carried through into many languages, with the names often reflecting the planetary association of that day. Even the Saxon deities whose names were attributed to four days of the week were based on their equation to the most comparable Roman planetary deities.

| | | | **Named After** | |
|---|---|---|---|---|
| **Planet** | **Days of the Week (English)** | **Days of the Week (Italian)** | **Roman Deity** | **Saxon Deity** |
| The Sun | Sunday | Domenica | Sol | |
| The Moon | Monday | Lunedì | Luna | |
| Mars | Tuesday | Martedì | Mars | Tiw |
| Mercury | Wednesday | Mercoledì | Mercury | Woden |
| Jupiter | Thursday | Giovedì | Jupiter | Thunor |
| Venus | Friday | Venerdì | Venus | Frigg |
| Saturn | Saturday | Sabato | Saturn | |

# Planetary Hours

*"I will speak of the unequal hours which are attributed unto the dominion or rule of the planets, for that the dominion of the hour serveth to the planets as for a dignity"*[12]

Although the idea that working with planetary hours has been promoted by some teachers as starting with the medieval grimoires, this is not the case. In ancient Egypt the Egyptian Priests attributed a different ruling god to each of the twenty-four hours of the day. The Greeks adopted this idea, rationalising it into the system we are now familiar with. They attributed the seven planets to the hours of the day, with the ruler of the first hour being the same as the ruler of the day[13] and through this they developed the system in which the repetitive sequence of the seven planets was first introduced.

If you are new to the concept of planetary hours you may at first be overwhelmed by the confusing use of the term *"hour"* for each time period as these are not the sixty-minute hours that we are accustomed to using in normal timekeeping. The planetary hours used in planetary magick are not the same as the sixty-minute hours beginning at midnight that we use for normal timekeeping. The planetary days are divided into twenty-four planetary hours starting with the first hour of the day beginning at sunrise and ending with the last hour of the day ending at sunrise of the next planetary day.

The period of daylight that extends from sunrise to sunset is divided into the twelve *"hours"* of the day. The period of darkness extending from sunset to sunrise of the next day is divided into the twelve *"hours"* of night. Combined these give the twenty-four hours of the planetary day. As the duration of daylight and darkness in a day will always differ except possibly at the Spring and Autumn Equinoxes when they may be equal, so on a particular planetary day the length of the hours of the day will differ from the

12 A Brief and most Easy Astrological Judgment of the Stars, Claudius Dariot, 1583

13 See The Exact Sciences in Antiquity, Neugebauer, 1967, p169.

length of the hours of the night. This is why the planetary hours are sometimes called the unequal hours. During the *"light"* half of the year between the Spring and Autumn Equinoxes there will be more hours of daylight than night, so the twelve planetary hours of the day will be longer than the twelve planetary hours of the night. The converse is true during the *"dark"* half of the year between the Autumn and Spring Equinoxes, when there are more hours of darkness than daylight and so correspondingly the twelve planetary hours of night are longer than those of the day.

Almanacs, ephemeredes and the internet are all sources you can use to discover the sunrise and sunset times, enabling you to calculate the planetary hours in advance and time your ceremonies appropriately.

## Attributions for Planetary Hours

| Planetary Hours of the Day | | | | | | | |
|---|---|---|---|---|---|---|---|
| **Hour** | **Sunday** | **Monday** | **Tuesday** | **Wednesday** | **Thursday** | **Friday** | **Saturday** |
| 1 | Sun | Moon | Mars | Mercury | Jupiter | Venus | Saturn |
| 2 | Venus | Saturn | Sun | Moon | Mars | Mercury | Jupiter |
| 3 | Mercury | Jupiter | Venus | Saturn | Sun | Moon | Mars |
| 4 | Moon | Mars | Mercury | Jupiter | Venus | Saturn | Sun |
| 5 | Saturn | Sun | Moon | Mars | Mercury | Jupiter | Venus |
| 6 | Jupiter | Venus | Saturn | Sun | Moon | Mars | Mercury |
| 7 | Mars | Mercury | Jupiter | Venus | Saturn | Sun | Moon |
| 8 | Sun | Moon | Mars | Mercury | Jupiter | Venus | Saturn |
| 9 | Venus | Saturn | Sun | Moon | Mars | Mercury | Jupiter |
| 10 | Mercury | Jupiter | Venus | Saturn | Sun | Moon | Mars |
| 11 | Moon | Mars | Mercury | Jupiter | Venus | Saturn | Sun |
| 12 | Saturn | Sun | Moon | Mars | Mercury | Jupiter | Venus |

| Planetary Hours of the Night | | | | | | | |
|---|---|---|---|---|---|---|---|
| **Hours** | **Sunday** | **Monday** | **Tuesday** | **Wednesday** | **Thursday** | **Friday** | **Saturday** |
| 1 | Jupiter | Venus | Saturn | Sun | Moon | Mars | Mercury |
| 2 | Mars | Mercury | Jupiter | Venus | Saturn | Sun | Moon |
| 3 | Sun | Moon | Mars | Mercury | Jupiter | Venus | Saturn |
| 4 | Venus | Saturn | Sun | Moon | Mars | Mercury | Jupiter |
| 5 | Mercury | Jupiter | Venus | Saturn | Sun | Moon | Mars |
| 6 | Moon | Mars | Mercury | Jupiter | Venus | Saturn | Sun |
| 7 | Saturn | Sun | Moon | Mars | Mercury | Jupiter | Venus |
| 8 | Jupiter | Venus | Saturn | Sun | Moon | Mars | Mercury |
| 9 | Mars | Mercury | Jupiter | Venus | Saturn | Sun | Moon |
| 10 | Sun | Moon | Mars | Mercury | Jupiter | Venus | Saturn |
| 11 | Venus | Saturn | Sun | Moon | Mars | Mercury | Jupiter |
| 12 | Mercury | Jupiter | Venus | Saturn | Sun | Moon | Mars |

## Calculations: Example 1

Let us say you wanted to work out the planetary hours for a ritual that focused on using Mercurial energies. Wednesday is the day of Mercury, so you decide to perform the ritual next Wednesday, during the day. The process is then as follows:

- ⊕ Consulting an almanac you see the sun rises at 7am on that day and sets at 8.48pm.
- ⊕ So the hours of daylight are from 07.00 – 20:48, giving 13 hours and 48 minutes.
- ⊕ 13 x 60 + 48 = 828 minutes of daylight.
- ⊕ Divide by 12 = 69.
- ⊕ This means each of the 12 "hours" of daylight will be 69 minutes long.

Consulting the tables given you see the first and eighth hours of Wednesday are ruled by Mercury. So for the first hour of the day the ritual should be performed between 7.00am and 8.09am (69 minutes).

For the eighth hour further calculation is needed:

- ⊕ Add together the "hour" length for 7 "hours" (7 x 69 = 483 minutes, or 8 hours and 3 minutes).
- ⊕ Then add this to the sunrise time (7:00am) + 8 hours and 3 minutes = 3:03pm).
- ⊕ This means the eighth hour starts at 3:03pm and finishes at 4:12pm (3:03 + 69 minutes).

You then decide which of these two times will be more practical, and you have your time to perform the ritual in.

## Calculations: Example 2

Let us say you now wanted to work out the planetary hours for a ritual that focused on using Saturnian energies. Saturday is the day of Saturn, so you decide to perform the ritual next Saturday, during the night when Saturn is visible in the sky. The process is then as follows:

Consulting an almanac you see the sun sets at 9.04pm on that day and rises the following morning at 6.10am.

- ⊕ So the hours of night are from 21.04 – 06:10, giving 9 hours and 6 minutes.
- ⊕ 9 x 60 + 6 = 546 minutes of night.
- ⊕ Divide by 12 = 45.5.
- ⊕ This means each of the 12 *"hours"* of the night will be 45.5 minutes long.

Consulting the tables given you see the third and tenth hours of Saturday night are ruled by Saturn. So if you now calculate these two times you have your options:

For the third hour

- ⊕ Sunset is 9.04pm so this is the base time you start from.
- ⊕ To calculate the start time for the third hour, add the *"hour"* length for 2 *"hours"* (2 x 45.5 = 91 minutes, or 1 hour and 31 minutes)
- ⊕ Add this to the sunset time (9.04) + 1 hour and 31 minutes = 10.35pm
- ⊕ The Saturnian hour runs from 10.35pm to 11.20.5pm (10.35 + 45.5 minutes)

For the tenth hour further calculation is needed:

- ⊕ Add together the "hour" length for 9 *"hours"* (9 x 45.5 = 409.5 minutes, or 6 hours and 49.5 minutes).
- ⊕ Then add this to the sunset time (9:04pm) + 6 hours and 49.5 minutes = 3:53.5am).
- ⊕ This means the tenth hour starts at 3:53.5am and finishes at 4:39am (3:53.5 + 45.5 minutes).

You then decide which of these two times will be more practical (probably 10.35pm!), and you have your time to perform the ritual in.

One further aspect you may wish to consider is the planetary movement. At times some of the planets go retrograde, i.e. appear to reverse their movement in the sky. This is taken in magickal terms to mean the energy is waning rather than waxing, so many magicians prefer to work when the planet is not retrograde. This can easily be checked by looking at an Astrological Ephemeris.

CHAPTER 6

# Invocation & Evocation

The grimoires placed a great deal of emphasis on interaction with spiritual creatures, either through invocation or evocation, or a combination of both. Invocation of a spiritual creature into a medium such as a crystal was a commonly used technique. This technique was used for most types of spiritual creature, including Archangels, demons, Olympic Spirits, Planetary Spirits, faeries and elementals. Confusingly, phrases such as *"Into this crystal stone or glass receptacle, or otherwise visibly out of the same"* are often to be found in grimoires, indicating that the call to the spiritual creature can result in invocation (into the crystal stone or glass receptacle) or evocation (*"visibly out of the same"*).

Evocation of a spiritual creature specifically to tangible appearance outside of a receptacle (i.e. without invocation) was almost always exclusively performed with demons. As the Planetary Spirits were also referred to as Planetary Demons, evocation was also used with them, which is why descriptions of their physical appearance and phenomenon associated with their appearance can be found in grimoires such as *Harley MSS 6482*, whereas physical descriptions are not given for the Planetary Intelligences, also known as Planetary Angels.

Such evocations were performed into a triangle, which acted as a cage to protect the summoner from the influence of the demon. The triangle usually had sides three foot long with protective divine names written around them, and was placed two foot from the outer edge of the circle in the direction the creature was expected to attend from. When demons were evoked in this manner, they would be bound through use of divine names of power to ensure their obedience and the truth of their statements and actions, as well as constraining them not to hurt any living thing or cause damage to the place.

*"And by the Seal of your Creation, being the mark, or Character of holiness unto you."*[14]

For both invocation and evocation, the magician would normally wear a lamen on their chest over their heart. This lamen would include the seal of the creature being called, which was believed to have the power to facilitate communication with the creature, as well as providing protection from the creature. It could also be seen as acting as a beacon for the creature on the physical plane, which when combined with the ceremony would tell it where to go to. For the Planetary Intelligences and Spirits these seals correspond to the sigils formed by sigilising their names on their appropriate planetary kameas (see Appendix 3). The lamen would be constructed during the appropriate planetary hour on the appropriate planetary day as part of the preparation for invocation or evocation. For the planetary archangels and demons, examples of their seals are found in different grimoires.

In addition to the lamen, the other main form of protection was the magick circle. A whole range of different magick circles are given in different grimoires, of varying complexity. The circle is usually nine foot in diameter, with a second circle within of eight foot diameter. What they usually have in common is pentagrams marking the four directions in the boundary between the two circles, and divine names between the four pentagrams. Both the pentagrams and divine names served as protection for the magician within the circle from any creature evoked outside of the circle. The pentagrams were drawn with the point of the pentagram facing inwards towards the centre of the circle. The divine names used were usually those considered particularly efficacious, such as Jahveh, Adonai, Eheia and Agla. Unlike the pentagrams the names were written facing inwards towards the magician in the centre. Within the circle at the centre was the altar, which was the focus for invocation as the place where the receptacle was positioned. The altar was

14 The Nine Keys, invocations to the archangels.

seen as sacred in itself, and often had its own circle drawn on it, within which the crystal would be placed.

For all works of planetary magick (and indeed any other magick) the practitioner should observe a principle which is stressed heavily in the grimoires, which is that of purification and consecration. All the tools used should be consecrated, as should talismans and amulets (see the section in the chapter on Amulets & Talismans). Purification also involves you, and this includes ritual bathing before any ceremony, and the mundane cleaning of the space you use as your temple for ceremonies on a regular basis. Anything you take into a magick circle for ritual work should have been purified. This includes mundane items you might not otherwise consider, such as your pair of glasses if you wear them.

The use of a series of conjurations to invoke or evoke a spiritual creature had a number of reasons. One was that it built up the energy and focused the attention of the magician. Another is that it might take time to draw the attention of the spiritual creature in question. Some writers have suggested that a series of conjurations implies a lack of belief that they will work, and the magician should only use the strongest conjuration. However this misses an obvious point, which can be best illustrated by analogy. If your telephone rings and you are not right next to it, it takes time for you to reach the telephone and answer it, assuming you are in the house. Like the ringing of the telephone, the conjurations draw the attention of the spiritual creature, and build up a magickal pressure encouraging it to answer your call. Of course if you are not in the house you cannot answer your telephone, so remember that if you are calling a unique spiritual creature, it is not impossible that it may already be somewhere fulfilling a task, in which case it is not going to respond to your call.

Binding a spiritual creature is also a part of the process of invocation and evocation. In this context the term binding should be clarified as the formalisation of an agreement, like a contract or oath, which the spiritual creature agrees to, to fulfil the task you have set it, and also to make subsequent contact easier. This may also include the spiritual creature giving the magician a particular seal to use to call it more easily, or a specific name to use to call it, as mentioned with the Olympic Spirits.

*"There are other names of the Olympic Spirits delivered by others; but they only are effectual, which are delivered to anyone, by the Spirit."*[15]

A component that is seen in both invocation and evocation is the license to depart. Having called a spiritual creature, when it had fulfilled the task it was called for, it was considered mandatory to license the creature to depart. This is not the same as banishing, as the context is entirely different. You banish unwanted influences or entities, and it would be incredibly rude to banish a spiritual creature you had summoned to assist you. This is why the licenses to depart found in the grimoires are courteous, though usually with a reminder that you might call on the creature's services again in the future.

Following the license to depart, a banishing or exorcism would then be performed. When calling a spiritual creature, it was considered akin to lighting a beacon, which could attract all manner of unwanted entities to the vicinity. Thus the performing of a banishing or exorcism would ensure that any unwanted *"guests"* would leave the vicinity and not cause any problems. In the case of demons, it was also thought that if the demon had become invisible after the license to depart, or had arrived but not assumed visible appearance and thus avoided being bound, and was still hanging around to cause mischief afterwards, you would be sending it away as well, preventing it from misbehaving.

---

15 Aphorism 18, Arbatel of Magick.

CHAPTER 7

# The Olympic Spirits

*"They are called Olympic Spirits, or Spirits of Olympus, which Inhabit in the Firmament, and in the Stars thereof, whose Office is to Declare the Fate and Destiny of Mortals, and to Administer Several other Matters and Things concerning our Terrestrial affairs; and to Teach and Declare those Things that the Stars to which every one is appointed, portendeth and Signifieth, according to the Doctrine of Astronomy and Astrology, wherein the Offices of the Olympic Spirits is most elegantly Set forth"*[16]

This seventeenth century description from *Rawlinson MSS D1363* of the Olympic Spirits gives an indication of their exalted nature. They are not simple spirits, but stellar governors who rule vast legions of spirits. The best way to describe them is probably as *"planetary governors"*, as the earliest reference to them in the sixteenth century *Arbatel of Magick* describes them in connection to spiritual governments and ruling provinces.

*"There are seven different governments of the Spirits of Olympus, by whom God hath appointed the whole frame and universe of this world to be governed."*[17]

The nearest spiritual creatures to which the Olympic Spirits could thus be compared are the archangels. Like the archangels they have a degree of autonomy, as seen by reference to their appearance. There is a similarity between the Olympic Spirits, with their consecutive periods of planetary rule through history of 490 years, and the planetary angels described by Johannes

16 MSS Rawlinson D1363

17 Aphorism 15, Arbatel of Magic

Trithemius in his work *De Septem Secundeis* (1508 CE), who consecutively rule for a period of 354 years and 4 months (and were in fact the archangels).

The Olympic Spirits, as the name *"Olympic"* suggests, are probably from Greek origins. For this reason they do not really fit well with the Hebrew hierarchy of spiritual creatures which is structured through its Qabalistic associations. It is also interesting to observe that unlike archangels which are considered to be made of the highest aspect of air, the Olympic Spirits are comprised of a balance of the four elements, indicating a much more physical sphere of influence.

This is an extremely important distinction, as all the spiritual creatures described from Hebrew sources, such as archangels, angels and demons, are all composed of a single element, usually air.

*"These Seven Imperial Princes, or Spiritual Governors,*
*with their Hosts, are in all the four Elements,*
*and do move with the equal Motion of the Firmament ,*
*and the Inferiors do always Depend upon,*
*and are Servient to the Superiors"*[18]

Reference made to the Olympic Spirits in *Harley MSS 6482*, a significant grimoire copied from seventeenth century material worked by the magician Dr Thomas Rudd, makes an important reference to the preference for working with the Olympic Spirits rather than the Hebrew orders of planetary spiritual creatures. This is a point we wish to emphatically emphasise, as the Olympic Spirits and their subservient spirits are far more accessible in many ways than archangels and angels.

*"To conclude Dr. Rudd's Doctrine of the Nine Hierarchies of Angels*
*and the better to understand him, that although the glorious Methratton*

---

18 MSS Rawlinson D1363

*and Raziel may be invocated for some great signal and weighty matters to prevent ruin of states and kingdoms and persons in great authority, yet it is the opinion of Dr. Dee and Dr. Rudd, and Iamblichus that ancient magician, that it is rarely practiced since the Olympic powers are sufficient to be invocated and advised with."*[19]

The qualities of the Olympic Spirits seem to be determined by the number seven, that of the classical planets. Thus we see that they all rule a number of provinces which is a multiple of seven, their period of rule is four hundred and ninety years each; and their sub-rulers are in multiples of seven.

| **Period of Rule** | | |
|---|---|---|
| **Planet** | **Governor** | **Period of Rule** |
| Jupiter | Bethor | 60 BC – 430CE |
| Mars | Phaleg | 431 CE – 920CE |
| Sun | Och | 921CE – 1410CE |
| Venus | Hagith | 1411CE – 1900CE |
| Mercury | Ophiel | 1901CE – 2390CE |
| Moon | Phul | 2391CE-2880CE |
| Saturn | Aratron | 2881CE – 3370 CE |

The current age is under the rule of Ophiel, the Mercurial Olympic Spirit, which is understandable in a world that has become so dominated by information technology.

19 MSS Harley 6482

**Olympic Spirit Rulerships**

| Planet | Governor | Provinces Ruled (Visible Provinces) | Number of Legions ( legion = 490 spirits) |
|---|---|---|---|
| Saturn | Aratron | 49 | 36 000 |
| Jupiter | Bethor | 32 | 29 000 |
| Mars | Phaleg | 35 | - |
| Sun | Och | 28 | 36 536 |
| Venus | Hagith | 21 | 4 000 |
| Mercury | Ophiel | 14 | 100 000 |
| Moon | Phul | 7 | - |
| | | 186 provinces | |

An important point mentioned in the *Arbatel of Magic* regarding the Olympic Spirits is that they do not always turn up when they are called. If the motives of the magician were not pure there was no guarantee of manifestation. And of course even if a spiritual creature did appear it might not be visible, which is why the grimoires place so much emphasis on thorough banishing even if nothing is obviously visible. This is why texts say that when called by a true magician who is acting in accord with the divine will, they are said to appear; however to a mean magician they send some of their spirits with limited powers, and to false magicians they do not appear at all but send demons instead.[20]

Also of course, it is possible that when you call an Olympic Spirit it may be otherwise occupied and send one of its many spirits from its legions to attend you rather than coming itself.

20 Aphorism 17, Arbatel of Magic

| Governor | Rules over |
| --- | --- |
| Aratron | 49 Kings, 42 Princes, 35 Presidents, 28 Dukes, 21 Ministers, Standing before him 14 familiars, 7 messengers |
| Bethor | 42 Kings, 35 Princes, 28 Dukes, 21 Counsellors, 14 Ministers, 7 Messengers |
| Phaleg | - |
| Och | Many subservients, yet he administreth all things alone and all his spirits serve him by centuries. |
| Hagith | Many subservient ministering spirits and over every 1000 he ordaineth Kings for their appointed seasons. |
| Ophiel | - |
| Phul | - |

| The Functions of the Olympic Spirits | | |
|---|---|---|
| **Planet** | **Olympic Spirit** | **Description** |
| Sun | Och | Och is called for treasure and wealth spells, being said to give gold and precious stones, and a *"purse springing with gold"*. He bestows wisdom and raises the dignity of a person so they are honoured and esteemed, so ideal for improving qualities of leadership and social position. His familiars are said to be excellent and teach perfect medicines, so ideal for healers. He is also said to prolong life. |
| Mercury | Ophiel | Ophiel teaches all subjects, he is the ideal spirit to call to help learn things. He gives familiar spirits. He is said to be able to make mercury transform into the Philosophers stone. |
| Venus | Hagith | Hagith increases personal beauty and attractiveness. He is said to transform copper to gold (and vice-versa). He gives faithful familiar spirits |
| Moon | Phul | Phul is a healer who can prolong life. He can transform all metals into silver. He gives undines as familiars. |
| Mars | Phaleg | Phaleg raises a person to great honour in matters of war. |
| Jupiter | Aratron | Aratron teaches alchemy, magick and healing. He is associated with transmutation, with his powers being given as converting anything into stone, and converting coal to treasure (and vice-versa). He causes the barren to become fruitful, and teaches invisibility. He gives long life. He gives familiars with a *"definite power"*, makes *"hairy men"* and can call subterranean spirits. |
| Saturn | Bethor | Bethor raises a person to great dignities, i.e. he should be called to when trying to gain promotion or improve your lot in life. He reveals treasures, and transports precious stones from place to place. He improves psychic powers, being said to make mediums work miraculous effects, and also ensure airy spirits give true answers. He prolongs life, and gives familiars of the firmament. |

**Olympic Spirit Seals & Astrological Rulerships**

| Planet | Spirit | Rulership | Seal |
|---|---|---|---|
| The Sun | Och | Leo | 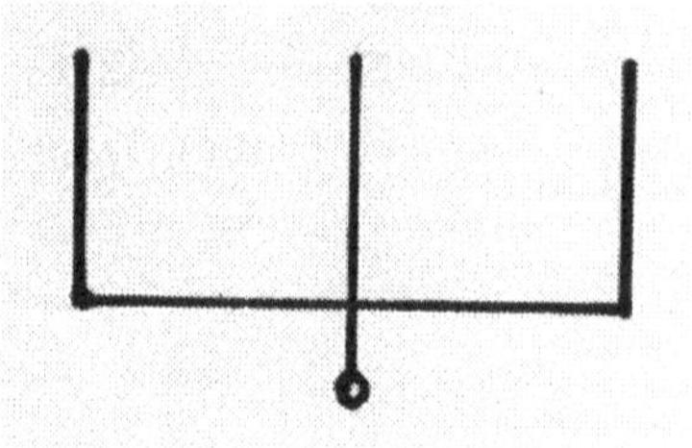 |
| Mercury | Ophiel | Gemini and Virgo | 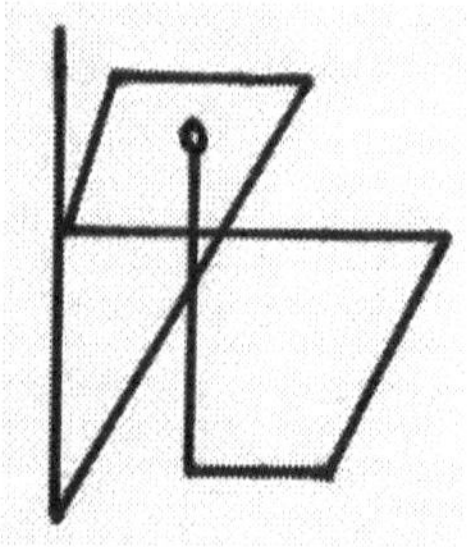 |
| Venus | Hagith | Libra and Taurus | 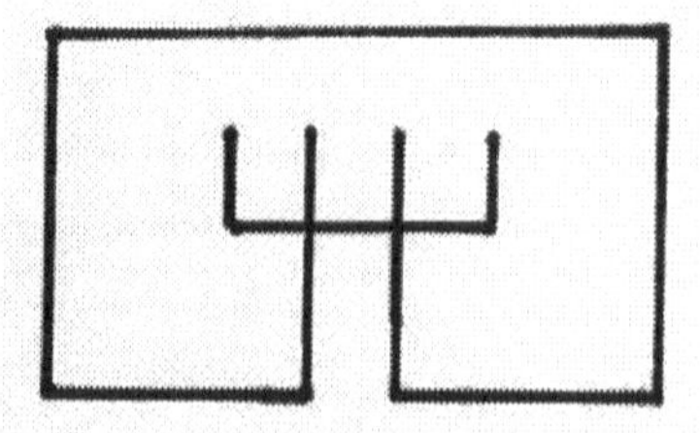 |

| Olympic Spirit Seals & Astrological Rulerships (continued) | | | |
|---|---|---|---|
| The Moon | Phul | Cancer | 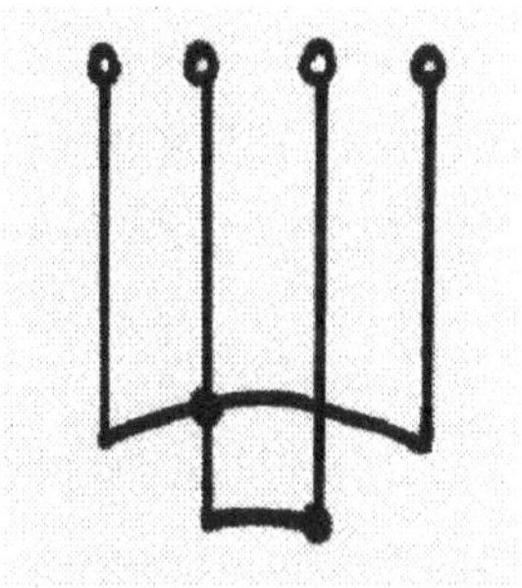 |
| Mars | Phaleg | Aries and Scorpio | 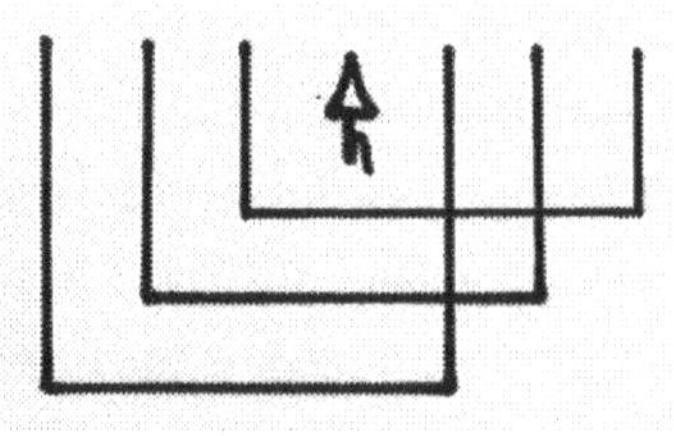 |
| Jupiter | Bethor | Pisces and Sagittarius | 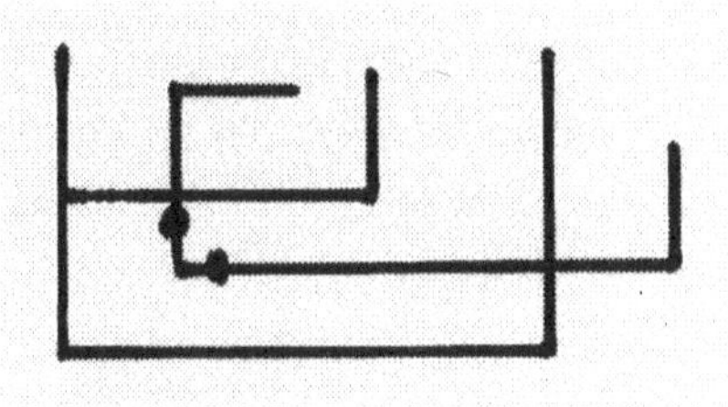 |
| Saturn | Aratron | Aquarius and Capricorn | 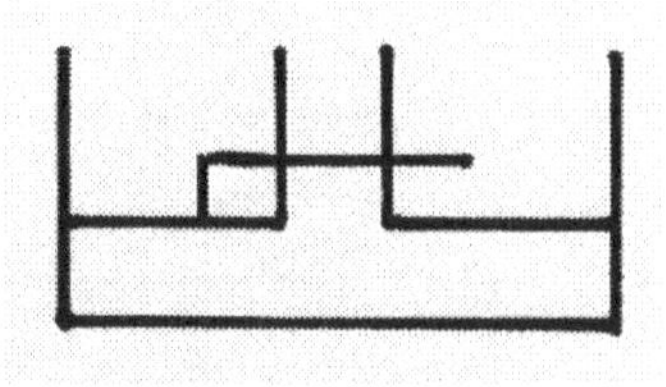 |

# Invoking the Olympic Spirits

*"There are other Names of the Olympic Spirits Delivered by tradition, but they only are Effectual which are delivered or Revealed to any One by the Spirit it Self, either visibly or invisibly; and they are Delivered to every One according as they Predestinated, or Sympathised, or are Governed by the Celestial Constellations in their Nativity, &c."*[21]

The first thing you need to do is decide which of the Olympic Spirits is appropriate for the operation you wish to undertake. Having determined this, you should work out the planetary hours for that Olympic Spirit on its day of the week. E.g. to call forth Bethor (Jupiter) it is best to do so on a Thursday during the planetary hour of Jupiter.

A talisman with the seal of the required Olympic Spirit should also be prepared before the operation. This you should prepare in a planetary magick circle, on the appropriate day and in the appropriate planetary hours for the spirit. The seal is placed under the crystal ball you use as a receptacle to call the Olympic Spirit into.

Hence you could prepare the seal in the first appropriate planetary hour of the appropriate day, and then do the invocation in the second appropriate planetary hour of the same day. The optimum Olympic Spirit for personal work is the one for the planet which rules your astrological sun-sign.

The sources give no details for preparation of space or tools to be used. The formula given is to first perform the preliminary conjuration, kneeling before the altar. Then stand and perform the main conjuration. Perform the active part of the ritual, making your request. This should all last no more than an hour. Then give the license to depart.

Obviously you should work out the wording of your request before you perform your ritual. Pay great attention to your request, examining and re-

---

21 MSS Rawlinson D1363

examining your words until you are totally happy with them. Remember spirits can be very literal in following instructions, and for this reason you should phrase your request very carefully. The golden rule is be precise and avoid ambiguity.

The structure for working with the Olympic Spirits is given in the *Arbatel of Magic,* first issued in 1575 CE in Basel. It was made available in English by Robert Turner as part of *The Fourth Book of Occult Philosophy* attributed to Agrippa, in 1655 CE. It is also to be found in *Rawlinson MSS D1363,* a seventeenth century manuscript. We have included the material found in both sources as the conjurations are identical (*Rawlinson MSS D1363* and *The Fourth Book of Occult Philosophy*), expanding and expounding where necessary to give a clear and coherent format to follow. We have chosen to leave the conjurations in their original form, which is why the language is archaic in style. However this archaic style has the benefit of forcing you to concentrate totally on what you are saying. If you prefer to you can rewrite them for your own purposes in modern English, using the original conjurations as a guideline for content.

As with any ritual, it is a good idea to have bathed beforehand as part of your purification process. Using an appropriate planetary scent in the bath will help the process of focusing your mind on the ritual to come. Likewise a period of meditation before you begin the ceremony is always worthwhile for the same reason.

## You will need:

- ⊕ A crystal or glass ball, preferably about 4" (10cm) in diameter.
- ⊕ The seal of the Olympic Spirit, ritually prepared beforehand.
- ⊕ A cloth or silk bag of the appropriate planetary colour.
- ⊕ A simple altar to place the seal and crystal onto.
- ⊕ An appropriately coloured planetary altar cloth.
- ⊕ An appropriately coloured planetary candle.
- ⊕ Censer with incense of an appropriate planetary nature.
- ⊕ A white robe.

**Note** - all of these items should have been consecrated previously before use. Candles should be new and unused.

## Altar Set-up:

The altar should have the altar cloth on it. The seal of the Olympic Spirit should be placed in the centre of the altar, underneath the crystal ball. The candle and censer may be placed on the floor at the edge of the circle (South for the candle and East for the censer), or they may be placed candle behind the crystal ball close to the edge of the altar, with the censer close by.

## The Ceremony:

Prepare the space by first lighting the candles and the incense.

Purify the space in your preferred manner, e.g. the Lesser Banishing Ritual of the Pentagram.

Perform the Heptagram ritual, using the invoking form for the planet associated with the Olympic Spirit you are calling.

Cast a Planetary Magick Circle.

Kneel before the altar and say the preliminary conjuration.

## Preliminary Conjuration:

*"O thou Almighty, Immaculate, Immortal and Incomprehensible God of Hosts, Creator of Heaven and Earth, who has spread the Heavens above the height of the Clouds, and Established the Waters upon the Earth, and appointed the Sea its Bounds, which it may not pass or exceed, and has placed the Sun, Moon, and Stars above the Air, in the Firmament of the Heavens, and who by your most excellent, Sacred, and Divine Wisdom, has placed all Creatures, both Celestial, Aerial, Terrestrial, and Infernal, to honour, obey, and glorify you in their Several & respective Orders, Offices, and Vocations; and made Man according to your own Similitude; and has ordained the whole Creation for your praise and Glory: O Lord, Illuminate my Understanding, enrich me with your Grace, fortify me with your Strength, protect me with your Shield, and Shadow me under the cover of your Celestial Wings, that the Envy, Malice, and Severity of no Person living, or any wicked Spirit, may have power to assault, hurt, or do me any injury or prejudice, but that I may vanquish and overcome all my Enemies, both private and public, visible and invisible, bodily and Ghostly.*

*And I beseech you, O most Gracious and Heavenly Lord God, that you would by your Divine Permission, cause to appear, and Send the Angel or Spirit N. of the [Saturnine, Jovial, Martial, Solar, Venereal, or, Mercurial] Order, [here nominating the particular Name of the Angel or Spirit, &c.] who shall Inform, Instruct, show forth, and teach me those things as I shall ask & desire of him, and to be friendly to me, and do for me as for your Servant, wherein Its Office is manifest, both now, and at all times, whensoever my necessity shall require Its Aid and Assistance. Which inestimable Boon I most humbly beg at your merciful Hands, Amen."*

Allow a couple of minutes, and then stand and declare the main conjuration.

## Conjuration:

*"O thou Celestial, Glorious, and Benevolent Angel: N: who are Principal Governor and bearing Imperial Rule, Power and Dominion over the [Saturnine, Jovial, Martial, Solar, Venereal, Mercurial, or, Lunar] Order of Angels, I call upon you, and most earnestly urge and entreat you in and through the Divine, Efficacious and Incomprehensible Name of the Eternal and Immense God, the Creator of Heaven and Earth – Jod Tetragrammaton; Hereby I urgently desire you to appear; and present yourself visibly unto me in this Crystal Stone, or otherwise to resolve for me what I shall ask of you, and to fulfil my humble requests in whatsoever I shall desire, according to your Office, or else to find, or raise to come, an Angel or Spirit from your Orders, authorised to fulfil my desires and petitions, as aforesaid. Move therefore, and show yourself in Power & Presence, Open the Mysteries of your Creation, be friendly unto me, for I am a servant of the same your God, the true worshipper of the Highest."*

You should now hopefully see the Olympic Spirit or one of its spirits in the crystal ball. At this point you should make your request to the Olympic Spirit, as you gaze into the crystal ball.

## Request:

When your request is finished, give the spirit the license to depart.

## License to Depart:

*"For as much as you came in Peace and Serenity, and have been friendly unto me, and answered my Petitions and Requests; I give thanks unto God, in whose name you came; and in whose Name, you may now at this time, depart in peace unto your Orders; always observing to return visibly to me again, at any time, and at all times, whensoever and wheresoever I shall call you, by your name, or by your Office, or by your Order, which is from the Beginning of your Election and Government primarily*

*Decreed and Ordained to you by the Omnipotent Creator of Heaven and Earth. Amen."*

Now place the seal in the cloth or silk bag of the appropriate planetary colour to be stored somewhere safe where nobody else will have access to it.

Perform the banishing version of the Heptagram ritual for the planet you were working with.

Perform any other banishing that may be appropriate to re-purify your space.

CHAPTER 8

# Qabalistic Spirits

In order to fully understand the scope of planetary work, especially when deciding to work with the various planetary spirits, intelligences and archangels, it is necessary to have a good understanding of the hierarchy of spiritual creatures. This will allow you to make the appropriate decisions as to which entity to call and work with in your ceremonies. Magickians during the Renaissance did not make the same distinctions as those which are commonly made in modern magick today. Over the last two or three decades, with the upsurge in interest in modern magickal and pagan practices, boundaries seems to have been erected through the pressure for individuals to make a decision as to which *"tradition"* they should follow and as such the rich heritage of spiritual creatures has become subdivided in a way that obstructs many from seeing the full picture.

The grimoire magicians of yesteryear did not make these distinctions and would have been as likely to work with fairies as they were angels, demons or planetary spirits. The whole body of grimoire magick was part of a unified corpus of magickal practice, and within this practice was a whole range of spiritual creatures. This is demonstrated by the same invocatory style being used to summon archangels, demons, Enochian governors, planetary spirits and Olympic spirits.

An example of this can be gleamed from *The Nine Keys* grimoire, which sets the Enochian System, of Dr. John Dee, within the context of the nine Orders of Angels, and also include various other orders of angels and spiritual creatures, giving a coherent hierarchy which makes for a clearer picture for working such grimoires. This hierarchy expands the nine Orders of Angels as they were set out by pseudo-Dionysus the Areopagite in his work *The Celestial Hierarchy* around 500 CE, which has been the accepted hierarchy of the angelic orders ever since.

As an aside, within the grimoires the Nine Orders Of Angels have different names to those used in Qabalah, resulting in some confusion, as e.g. the Seraphim in the grimoires correspond to the Chaioth haQadosh of the Qabalah, whereas the Seraphim of the Qabalah correspond to the order of Potestates or Powers in the grimoires. The Kabbalistic roots of the planetary spiritual creatures in this hierarchy will now be considered.

**Planetary Hierarchy**

| Heaven | Planet | Archangel | Order of Angels | Intelli-gences | Spirit |
|---|---|---|---|---|---|
| **Superior Hierarchy** | | | | | |
| | | Metatron | Seraphim | | |
| | | Raziel | Cherubim | | |
| 7 | Saturn | Tzaphkiel | Thrones | Agiel | Zazel |
| **Middle Hierarchy** | | | | | |
| 6 | Jupiter | Tzadkiel | Dominations | Jophiel | Hismael |
| 5 | Mars | Khamael | Powers | Graphiel | Bartzabel |
| 4 | Sun | Michael | Virtues | Nakhiel | Sorath |
| **Inferior Hierarchy** | | | | | |
| 3 | Venus | Uriel | Principalities | Hagiel | Kedemel |
| 2 | Mercury | Raphael | Archangels | Tiriel | Taphthartharath |
| 1 | Moon | Gabriel | Angels | Malka[22] | Schad |

The Hebrew attributions to the planets date back to the roots of the Jewish Kabbalah, and were subsequently reinforced by the synthesis of

22 Malka is commonly used as shorthand for Malka be-Tharshisim ve-ad Be-Ruachoth Shechalim

Kabbalistic material into the grimoires with their largely planetary focus during the Middle Ages and Renaissance. At first glance the seven classical planets might not seem a good fit onto the ten Sephiroth of the Tree of Life, but there is a long tradition and history of planetary associations with the Kabbalah.

The planetary influence in Kabbalah can be seen in both the schools which combined to form the later practices, *Maaseh Merkavah* (*"Workings of the Chariot"*) with its emphasis on the first chapter of *Ezekiel*, and *Maaseh Bereshith* (*"Workings of the Beginning"*), which was focused around the cosmology and cosmogony of the first chapter of *Genesis* as a revelatory text.

These need to be considered in turn to see the planetary influence in each of them. The word *Merkavah* means *"chariot"*, and refers to the vision of Ezekiel's chariot found in the *Book of Ezekiel* in the Bible. The texts relating to Merkavah Mysticism are commonly referred to as *Hekhalot* texts. Hekhalot means *"hall"* or *"chamber"*, and is used to denote the seven planetary palaces through which the practitioner of Merkavah would pass to enter into the presence of God.

The Merkavah Mystic or Rider sought entry into the throne world of God, using fasting and repetitious use of hymns and prayers, akin to mantra. When in trance he would send his spirit upwards through the Seven Palaces, using magickal amulets and long memorized incantations to ensure successful passage past the guardian angels and demons he would encounter. The Merkavah cosmology is specifically planetary, focusing on the Sephiroth which correspond to the seven classical planets, from Yesod the Sephira of the Moon up to Binah the Sephira of Saturn.

Considering the images of the Greco-Roman gods as riding chariots (such as Sol and Luna in their chariots travelling through the day and night skies respectively), it is interesting to note the significance of the chariot in this form of early mysticism and speculate as to the level of cross-fertilisation of ideas that may have occurred. Echoes of the Merkavah tradition can be found throughout the medieval grimoires, from the use of planetary amulets and long invocations, through to the purificatory use of fasting and prayers. Even references to the *"chariot of the soul"* can be found in some grimoires.

If we now consider the Maaseh Bereshith school of Kabbalah, the planetary influence is again pronounced. One of the earliest and greatest of Jewish Kabbalistic texts, the *Sepher Yetzirah* (*"Book of Formation"*) was written in the first or second century CE. In this text, the fourth of the sixth chapters focuses on the sevenfold associations of the planets and their connection to the Hebrew alphabet and Kabbalistic symbolism.

*"Seven Doubles: ....*
*And with them He formed,*
*Seven planets in the Universe,*
*Seven days in the Year,*
*Seven gates in the Soul, male and female."*[23]

The seven doubles are the seven double letters of the Hebrew alphabet, so-called because there are two ways of pronouncing each letter depending on their position in a word. The seven double letters correspond to the planetary Sephiroth on the Tree of Life. The seven planetary Sephiroth also directly relate to the days of the week, as described in creation (i.e. the *Book of Genesis*).

The six planetary Sephiroth of Yesod, Hod, Netzach, Tiphereth, Geburah and Chesed correspond to the days from Sunday to Friday and are collectively known as *Sephiroth ha-Benyin* (*"the Sephiroth of Construction"*), with the Saturnian Sephira of Binah corresponding to the Sabbath, which takes its name from the Hebrew word for Saturn, *"Shabathai"*. From this sevenfold symbolism a whole range of other associated qualities are used in Kabbalah, including the concept of the *"Cube of Space"*, with the six directions and the centre corresponding to the planets. Thus the planetary energies are associated with both time and space. These qualities have been changed in

---

23 Sepher Yetzirah 4:6.

later Western mystery Tradition Qabalah to be more in line with classical influences, but clearly show the significance of planetary symbolism to the development of early Kabbalah and its derivatives.

The different types of Qabalistic spiritual creatures associated with the planets and when to work with them can be very confusing. The archangels associated with the planets are like overseers, directing the energy of the planets, and in this sense could be seen as lenses for their respective planetary energies. You call on the archangels when you want to direct a particular planetary energy into your ceremony. This can be for any form of planetary magick.

The Planetary Intelligences, also known as Planetary Angels, embody the positive qualities of their respective planets, and act as managers for the planetary spirits. The Planetary Spirits, also known as Planetary Demons, are comprised of ungoverned pure planetary energy without focus, and should always be directed by the appropriate Planetary Intelligence or Archangel when used.

Both the Planetary Intelligences and Spirits are usually only called on for the making and empowering of amulets and talismans. This is clearly seen by the fact that the numerical totals for the names of the Planetary Intelligences and Planetary Spirits all add up to a total equating to an aspect of the appropriate planetary magick number square (kamea), such as the sum of the numbers in the square, the sum of a row, or the number of squares in the kamea.

Thus the Planetary Intelligences of Saturn, Jupiter, Mars and the Moon add to the same as the kamea total; Sun and Mercury to the row total; and Venus to the number of squares. In the case of the Planetary Spirits, those of Saturn, Jupiter, Mars, Sun, Mercury and Moon add to the same as the kamea total; and Venus to the row total.

# The Spiritual Creatures of the Sun

| | |
|---|---|
| **Archangel** | Michael |
| **Rules the** | Malakhim / Order of Virtues |
| **In the** | Fourth Heaven of Sol |
| **Under the Divine Name** | Eloha |
| **He is also called** | Shemeliel, Schemeshiel, Soliah |
| **Planetary Spirit** | Sorath |
| **Planetary Intelligence** | Nakhiel |
| **Order of Demons** | Aerial Powers |

## Archangel: Michael

Michael was the first angel created, and is often seen as the leader of the angels or *"first among equals"*. His name means *"He who is like God"*. He is usually shown wielding a sword or lance, and sometimes the scales of justice. As with the other archangels, Michael should be visualised standing about 3m tall, and he wears a golden yellow tunic.

Michael is the archangel of Fire and the Sun, and helps those who call him to achieve goals and destinies. Amongst the achievements especially sacred to Michael are marriage and music. If you are seeking to achieve a legitimate goal, or in need of protection, Michael is the angel you should call to, as he is the defender of the just and is also known as the Merciful Angel.

Michael appears a number of times in the Bible. Michael was the archangel who appeared to Moses as the fire in the burning bush. He also rescued Daniel from the lion's den and informed Mary of her approaching death. Michael appears in Revelations as the leader of the celestial host that defeats the antichrist. He is the prayer-leader in the Heavens in Islam.

## Order of Angels: Malakhim

The Solar Order of Angels is called by two different names. In the Grimoires they are called the Virtues, and in Qabalah they are called the Malakhim (*"Kings"*). For consistency we are using the Qabalistic names for the Orders of Angels. The Malakhim should be called upon to strengthen the will, courage, humility and patience, and aid the caller in coping with adversity and trauma. In appearance the Malakhim stand about 2m tall, and are very beautiful. They have white wings, and wear golden tunics and have golden crowns on their heads. All around them there is an intense aura of nobility and grace.

## Planetary Intelligence: Nakhiel

Nakhiel is good for gaining success and elevation. He also helps with having speedy journeys, and bringing people to you quickly that you want to see. Nakhiel responds to the Divine Names: Elah (ALH), El (AL), Elban (ALBN).

## Planetary Spirit: Sorath

Sorath has a large and full body or great stature. His skin is reddish with a gold tinge. He moves swiftly, as lightning. The sign of his appearance is a tendency for the magician to start sweating.

# The Spiritual Creatures of Mercury

| | |
|---|---|
| **Archangel** | Raphael |
| **Rules the** | Bene Elohim / Order of Archangels |
| **In the** | Second Heaven of Mercury |
| **Under the Divine Name** | Elohim Tzabaoth |
| **He is also called** | Cochabiel, Cochalijah, Mercuriel |
| **Planetary Spirit** | Taphthartharath |
| **Planetary Intelligence** | Tiriel |
| **Order of Demons** | Sifters, Tryers or Accusers, Inquisitors |

## Archangel: Raphael

Raphael means *"Healer of God"*, and he is the archangel charged with healing mankind and the earth. He is the Archangel of Mercury and the Air. He is the patron of travellers, often being depicted with a pilgrim's staff, and he protects those on journeys, especially air travel. As well as protecting travellers, Raphael's special charges are the young and innocent. Raphael is the archangel of knowledge and communication, and may be called to help with any related areas, such as improving your memory, learning languages, exams, dealing with bureaucracy and business matters.

Raphael was the angel who gave King Solomon the ring inscribed with the pentagram that enabled him to bind demons, and force them to build his temple. He was said to have healed the earth after the Flood, and also visited Noah after the Flood to give him a book of medicine, which had belonged to the angel Raziel. Raphael is usually seen standing about 3m tall, with a beautiful face. He wears an orange robe and sandals, and may bear a caduceus in his right hand.

## Order of Angels: Bene Elohim

In the Grimoires the Mercurial Order of Angels is called the Archangels, whereas the same order is known as Bene Elohim (*"Sons of Gods"*) in Qabalah. They are both names for the same beings. It is easier to use the name Bene Elohim, as the name Archangels for an Order of Angels can cause confusion with the individual beings called Archangels, who are higher in the hierarchy and rule the Orders of Angels. The Bene Elohim should be called upon to strengthen the mind and intuition, increase precognition and spiritual devotion. In appearance the Bene Elohim stand about 2m tall with white wings and are very beautiful. Some of them appear more masculine, and some more feminine. They wear orange tunics.

## Planetary Intelligence: Tiriel

Tiriel is good for improving learning and knowledge, and giving eloquence of speech. He is good for divination, especially by dream. He helps avoid poverty and makes a person sociable and easy to get on with. Tiriel responds to the Divine Names: Din (DIN), Doni (DNI), Asboga (ASBVGA).

## Planetary Spirit: Taphthartharath

Taphthartharath has a medium size body and an attractive face. He appears as an armed knight in armour. He moves like the clouds. The sign of his appearance is a feeling of fear or nervousness.

# The Spiritual Creatures of Venus

| | |
|---|---|
| **Archangel** | Uriel |
| **Rules the** | Elohim / Order of Principalities |
| **In the** | Third Heaven of Venus |
| **Under the Divine Name** | Yahveh Tzabaoth |
| **He is also called** | Nogathiel, Oriel, Vendriel |
| **Planetary Spirit** | Kedemel |
| **Planetary Intelligence** | Hagiel |
| **Order of Demons** | Furies, Seminaries of Evil |

## Archangel: Uriel

Uriel, also known as Auriel or Oriel, is the Archangel of Venus and of Earth, and of peace and salvation. His name means *"Light of God"*, and he is often depicted with a flame or lamp in his hands. Uriel embodies the power of light as illumination and spiritual passion. Uriel is associated with magical power, and the application of force. As such he is the angel to help cause a positive breaking of bonds when needed and overcoming inertia, being able to go with the flow of the *"winds of change"*. He is also the patron of astrology and has been linked strongly with electricity.

Uriel is credited with being the angel who gave alchemy and the Qabalah to man. Uriel was the angel who helped inspire Abraham to lead the Jews out of Ur. As one of the most powerful archangels, Uriel is said to be the bearer of the keys to hell, standing as guardian to that infernal realm. Uriel is usually seen standing about 3m tall, with a beautiful face. He wears an emerald green robe and carries a copper lamp in his left hand.

## Order of Angels: Elohim

The Venusian Order of Angels is known by two different names. In the Grimoires they are called the Principalities, and in Qabalah they are the Elohim (*"Gods"*). The Elohim should be called upon to improve your personal situation so you can more effectively fulfil your spiritual path, and also how to handle power so it is not abused but used positively. The Elohim are seen as standing about 2m tall, with white wings and are very beautiful. Some have more masculine faces and some more feminine. They wear emerald green tunics and are surrounded by an aura of beauty.

## Planetary Intelligence: Hagiel

Hagiel is good for ending strife. He is also called to help gain love and enable conception free from barrenness. He can also diffuse enchantments. Hagiel responds to the Divine Names: Shaddai (ShDI), Dagail (DGAIL).

## Planetary Spirit: Kedemel

Kedemel has an attractive body or medium size, with an attractive face. His skin is white with a green tinge, and may have also a golden hue. He moves as a star through the heavens. The sign of his appearance is noise like women playing outside the circle.

# The Spiritual Creatures of the Moon

| | |
|---|---|
| **Archangel** | Gabriel |
| **Rules the** | Kerubim / Order of Angels |
| **In the** | First Heaven of Luna |
| **Under the Divine Name** | Shaddai |
| **He is also called** | Jorvahol, Levanael, Lounael, Lunajah |
| **Olympic Spirit** | Phul |
| **Planetary Spirit** | Chasmodai |
| **Planetary Spirit of Spirits** | Schad Barschemoth ha-Shartathan |
| **Planetary Intelligence** | Malka be-Tharshisim ve-ad Be-Ruachoth Shechalim |
| **Order of Demons** | Tempters, Ensnarers |

## Archangel: Gabriel

Gabriel means *"The Strength of God"*. Gabriel is the angel who usually delivers messages to humanity, embodying the link between man and the universe and the divine as expressed by the Moon. Gabriel first appears in the Old Testament in the book of Daniel. It is Gabriel who first indicates the coming of a messiah to Daniel in this book. Gabriel visited Zachary to tell him his son would be called John (the Baptist) and most famously he told Mary that she was pregnant with Jesus. In Islam Gabriel is also seen as the divine messenger, it was he who delivered the *Qur'an* to Mohammed.

As the Archangel of the Moon and Water, Gabriel is the guide to the inner tides of our unconscious. Gabriel can help with developing the imagination and psychic abilities. He is also associated with domestic matters, especially the development of the home, or finding a new home. Gabriel is the archangel to call to if you are having problems with your menstrual cycle, as he rules the forces that influence it.

Gabriel can appear as male or female, and may be called to as either. Gabriel often appears carrying a staff topped with lilies, showing his fruitful nature and ability to help you bring plans to fruition. He is usually seen standing about 3m tall, with a beautiful face, which is more feminine than most of the archangels. He wears a violet robe, and may bear a silver cup in his hands.

## Order of Angels: Kerubim

The lunar Order of Angels is another one which has different names. In the Grimoires they are called the Angels, and in Qabalah they are called the Kerubim (*"The Strong"*). Again the Qabalistic name is easier to use, as the name Angels is also a generic and can cause confusion. It should be noted that in the Grimoires the name Kerubim is used for the Order of Angels associated with the Zodiac, which are called the Auphanim (*"Wheels"*) in Qabalah. Nonetheless as we are using the Qabalistic convention for this work, the Kerubim is applied to the lunar Order of Angels. The Kerubim should be called upon for sustenance through troubles, and for guidance in dealing with immediate problems.

The Kerubim are the most elemental of the Orders of Angels, and are probably the easiest to contact for this reason. The elemental nature of the Kerubim is seen in their appearance. They have two sets of wings, one set pointing upwards and one set downwards; and each has a head of one of the four elemental animals – eagle, lion, man and bull.

## Planetary Intelligence of Intelligences: Malka

Malka be-Tharshisim ve-ad Be-Ruachoth Shechalim is often shortened simply to Malka for convenience. Malka helps a person be happy and affable, and improves body health. He also increases riches and drives away enemies. Malka responds to the Divine Names: Hod (HVD), Elim (ALM), Eliha (ALIH).

## Planetary Spirit: Chasmodai

Chasmodai is described as the Planetary Spirit of the Moon, yet there is no information about him.

## Planetary Spirit of Spirits: Schad Barschemoth ha-Shartathan

Schad Barschemoth ha-Shartathan (often referred to as *Schad* for convenience) has a large body with soft blackish skin. He has red, watering eyes and is bald, with sharp teeth. He moves like a tempest at sea. The presence of water outside the circle is a sign of his appearance.

# The Spiritual Creatures of Mars

| | |
|---|---|
| **Archangel** | Khamael |
| **Rules the** | Seraphim / Order of Potestates (Powers) |
| **In the** | Fifth Heaven of Mars |
| **Under the Divine Name** | Elohim Gibor |
| **He is also called** | Camael, Madimiel, Martiel, Samael, Zamael |
| **Planetary Spirit** | Bartzabel |
| **Planetary Intelligence** | Graphiel |
| **Order of Demons** | Jugglers and Deluders |

## Archangel: Khamael

Khamael is the archangel of Mars, and is one of the seven archangels who stand in the presence of god, which is emphasized by the meaning of his name, *"He who sees God"*. Khamael is a warrior who represents divine justice, and is the head of the order of Angels called Seraphim.

In appearance Khamael stands about 3m tall with a beautiful face and fiery red hair. He appears as a warrior, with a scarlet red tunic, green plates of armour, an iron helmet and a sword. He has large green wings.

Khamael is said to grant invisibility and rules over martial qualities like power and invincibility. Khamael is the ideal angel to call upon to help you take personal responsibility and to develop self-confidence. He will help you deal with the consequences of your actions and to find justice, but only if you stick to the truth. Many writers have put Khamael forward as the angel who wrestled with Jacob. He is also thought to have been the other angel who appeared with Gabriel to comfort Jesus during his agony in the garden of Gethsemane.

Khamael is the angel who guards the gates of heaven, chief of the 12,000 fiery Angels of destruction who guard the gates. Khamael is also the angel who holds Leviathan in check until Judgement Day, when he will swallow the souls of sinners. Other duties of Khamael are as patron Angel of all those who love God, governing the heavenly singing, and to bring the gift of godliness to mankind, helping them find the holiness that exists within but is rarely fully released.

## Order of Angels: Seraphim

The Martial Order of Angels is known in the Grimoires as the Potestates or Powers, and in Qabalah as the Seraphim (*"Fiery Serpents"*). This is confusing as in the Grimoires the name Seraphim is used for a different Order of Angels, which corresponds to the Qabalistic Chaioth haQadosh (*"Holy Living Creatures"*) attributed to the highest Sephira of Kether. However as this is not a planetary sphere, and we are using the convention of the Qabalistic names, we are referring to the Martial Order of Angels as the Seraphim. The Seraphim should be called upon for spiritual protection from negative influences or entities, and for overcoming passions or negative emotions which are detrimental to your growth. In appearance the Seraphim are very beautiful angels, around 2m tall with who have three pairs of white wings on their backs, in scarlet tunics, whose auras are filled with flames that surround them at all times.

## Planetary Intelligence: Graphiel

Graphiel is very good for winning conflicts, to the extent of bringing those in conflict to you from wherever they are. He is also used to stop the flow of blood. Graphiel responds to the Divine Names: Adonai (ADNI), Melek (MLK), Eheia (AHIH).

## Planetary Spirit: Bartzabel

Bartzabel is tall with a dirty face. He has a dark skin, or red, with stag horns and claws, and moves swiftly like burning fire. The sign of his arrival is unexpected noise around the circle.

# The Spiritual Creatures of Jupiter

| | |
|---|---|
| **Archangel** | Tzadkiel |
| **Rules the** | Chasmalim / Order of Dominations |
| **In the** | Sixth Heaven of Jupiter |
| **Under the Divine Name** | El |
| **He is also called** | Cassiel, Joviel, Satqiel, Zabdiel, Zabkiel, Zachariel, Zachiel, Zadkiel, Zedekiel, Zedkiel |
| **Planetary Spirit** | Hismael |
| **Planetary Intelligence** | Jophiel |
| **Order of Demons** | Avengers of Wickedness |

## Archangel: Tzadkiel

Tzadkiel is the archangel of Jupiter, and of benevolence, memory and mercy. His name means *"Righteousness of God"*, and he is often depicted with a dagger in his hand. However this dagger represents the power of the intellect, and also his role in saving Abraham's son. Tzadkiel is a comforter, and he is associated with invocation and prayer. He is hence the archangel to help overcome despondency, and to help you forgive others for their negative deeds.

Through prayer and invocation he is also a channel to help you attune yourself with divinity in the way you perceive and experience it. As archangel of Jupiter, Tzadkiel can also be appealed to for help with financial matters and for achieving justice in a situation. Tzadkiel is the angel who prevents Abraham from sacrificing his young son Isaac to God, which is where his associations with the dagger and mercy come from.

Tzadkiel is the chief of the order of angels known as the Brilliant Ones (Chasmalim). He is one of the two standard bearers (along with Zophiel) who follow directly behind Michael as he enters battle. Tzadkiel is described as one of the seven archangels who preside next to God. Tzadkiel is usually seen standing about 3m tall, with a beautiful face, wearing a blue tunic and bearing a dagger in his left hand.

## Order of Angels: Chasmalim

The Jupiterian Order of Angels is called the Dominions or Dominations in the Grimoires, and the Chasmalim (*"Brilliant Ones"*) in Qabalah. The Chasmalim should be called upon for focusing your will, and refining your senses, as well as resisting strong temptations which are not beneficial to your development (though they may appeal to your hedonistic side). The Chasmalim stand about 2m tall, and are extremely beautiful, with white wings. They wear sapphire blue tunics, and give off an aura of intense light that makes it difficult to look at them.

## Planetary Intelligence: Jophiel

Jophiel (*"Beautiful One of God"*) has the powers of assisting to gain favour with powerful people, and appeasing enemies. He is also very good for dealing with difficult situations and for disclosing lies and illusions. Jophiel responds to the Divine Names: El (AL), Ab (AB), Abab (ABAB), IHVH (Yahveh).

## Planetary Spirit: Hismael

Hismael has a body of medium stature and a mild face, with reddish skin. He moves quickly, as with the flashings of lightning and thunder. The sign of his arrival is glimpses of movement as of men moving around the circle.

# The Spiritual Creatures of Saturn

| | |
|---|---|
| **Archangel** | Tzaphkiel |
| **Rules the** | Aralim / Order of Thrones |
| **In the** | Seventh Heaven of Saturn |
| **Under the Divine Name** | Yahveh Elohim |
| **He is also called** | Captiol, Cassiel, Jophiel, Orifiol, Sabathiel, Saturniel, Zaphkiel |
| **Planetary Spirit** | Zazel |
| **Planetary Intelligence** | Agiel |
| **Order of Demons** | Vessels of Iniquity |

## Archangel: Tzaphkiel

The Saturnian archangel is Tzaphkiel whose name means *"Beholder of God"*. Tzaphkiel is one of the seven archangels who stand in the presence of God. He is known as the Angel of Paradise because of his role in the Garden of Eden, and in modern times is the patron of all those who fight pollution and love and protect nature.

Tzaphkiel is also the patron of artists, bringing illumination and inspiration to those who seek to create beauty in the world. He is usually seen as a beautiful male angel standing about 3m tall, wearing a black tunic, with white wings, and bearing a flaming sword in his right hand.

He is the first angel mentioned in the Bible, though not by name, being the guardian of the Tree of Life, and it was he who drove Adam and Eve from the Garden of Eden after they had eaten the forbidden apple, and bars the return of man, standing at the gates bearing the flaming sword. Tzaphkiel is one of the chiefs of the choirs of the Cherubim, who are assigned the task of watching the four gates to Eden. He is also a Prince of the Angelic Order of Thrones. Tzaphkiel is said in Jewish lore to be especially good friends with Metatron, the archangel of Kether who is the voice of God.

## Order of Angels: Aralim

The Saturnian Order of Angels is called the Thrones in the Grimoires, and the Aralim (*"Strong and Mighty Ones"*) in Qabalah. The Aralim should be called upon to help you make correct judgments, especially when faced with difficult choices and no obvious solutions. In appearance the Aralim stand about 2m tall, with beautiful though somewhat severe faces. They wear black tunics and gold crowns. They have white wings on their backs, and rainbows play about them at all times.

## Planetary Intelligence: Agiel

Agiel is associated with safe births, for both mother and child, and also the same for animals. He is also called to prevent miscarriage during pregnancy. He is also good for petitions to powerful people, which can be interpreted as job applications, court cases, etc. Agiel responds to the Divine Names: Ab (AB), Hod (HVD), Yah (IH), Hod (HVD), IHVH (Yahveh).

## Planetary Spirit: Zazel

Zazel has a tall, lean and slender body. He has four faces on his head, facing in each direction. He also has a black shining face on each knee. He moves like the wind driven by an earthquake. The sign of his arrival is whiteness around the circle.

# Planetary Intelligences

*"There are Seven Intelligences or Spirits, of light, who are Celestially Dignified, by nature, Angelical & Benevolent, whose names are to be Collected, & Characters Drawn from the forementioned tables[24]; with the names of God, Governing them, by the force, Influence, Virtue, & Mystical, & Secret, Efficacy, whereof, them good demons, are powerfully moved, & to be Called forth, to Visible Appearance, whose Names are as followeth."*[25]

The Planetary Intelligences, or Planetary Angels as they are also known, are directors of planetary energy. They are benevolent spiritual creatures, who govern the undirected and amoral force of the Planetary Spirits. Their seals are often used on talismans to act as a focus for the planetary energy, together with the Planetary Spirits.

The Planetary Intelligences (and Spirits) are first found in Agrippa's *Three Books of Occult Philosophy,* which though published in 1531-3 CE, was first drafted around 1508-9 CE. It is unlikely that Agrippa made them up, and he probably heard about them from his teacher, the extremely significant magickal figure Abbot Johannes Trithemius. However the source of their origin is currently a mystery.

Should you decide at some point that you wish to try invoking the Planetary Intelligences, an old Conjuration from a grimoire is included as Appendix 12 of this volume and you may want to study it, using it as it is presented or adapting it for your personal use. The style of practice given for the Olympic Spirits may be used, substituting the Planetary Intelligence Invocation for the main Conjuration, and adjusting the other components appropriately to change any references to the Olympic Spirit to that of the appropriate Planetary Intelligence.

---

24 This is a reference to the planetary kameas.

25 Sloane MSS 3821

# Manifestation of Spiritual Creatures

Renaissance Magickians recorded the results they obtained whilst working with the spiritual creatures associated with the seven classical planets and for the purposes of your own comparison, should you decide to perform evocation or indeed meditations or contemplations with these beings we include the common forms recorded for each planet here.

| | |
|---|---|
| **The Sun** | A King with a sceptre riding on a lion, a crowned King, a Queen with a sceptre, a bird, a lion, a cock, a yellow or golden garment and a sceptre. |
| **Mercury** | Classic Mercurial symbols such as the fair youth (Hermes or Mercury), the magpie and a robe of changeable colours. Other manifestations described are a King riding upon a bear, a woman holding a distaff, a dog, a she bear, a rod and a little staff |
| **Venus** | Images of the beautifully dressed and clothed maid (Venus), A King with a sceptre riding upon a camel, a She-Goat, Camel or Dove. Flowers and garments in the colours white or green are also often cited. |
| **The Moon** | Classical image of a female huntress with a bow and arrows (Artemis/Diana), as well as the arrow itself and the colour silver. Lunar spirits may also appear as a King riding on a Doe, a little boy, a cow, a little doe, a goose, a creature with many feet or in the form of green or silver coloured garments. |
| **Mars** | Includes symbols such as weapons, the wolf and the colour red. Spirits associated with Mars may also appear as an armed King riding upon a wolf, an armed man, a woman holding a buckler on her thigh, a goat, a horse, a stag, wool or as red garments. |
| **Jupiter** | A man wearing a mitre in a long robe, a maid with a laurel crown, adorned with flowers, a bull, stag or peacock. It may also manifest as a sword, a box tree or as an azure coloured garment. |
| **Saturn** | Includes a King with a beard seen riding on a Dragon, an old man with a beard, an old woman leaning on a staff, a hog, a Dragon, an owl, a black garment, a hook or sickle or as a Juniper tree. |

**CHAPTER 9**

# Kamea Sigilisation

A sigil is a pictographic representation of the name of a spiritual creature or of your intent. When you use a sigil representing a spiritual creature you are creating a gateway for the energy of that creature to manifest. When you draw a sigil of this sort onto an amulet or talisman, you are creating a link to the spiritual creature to enable energy to be drawn from it, like charge from a battery. The sigils for planetary spiritual creatures are created by drawing them out on kameas.

Kameas are planetary magick number squares whose row and column length corresponds to the associated number for the planet, e.g. Saturn has a 3x3 square, Jupiter a 4x4 square etc. Magick number squares are figures where the total for every row, column and diagonal in the square is the same. There are different mathematical formulae for generating such magick number squares, and the kameas were created using one of these formulae. The kameas generated in this way then became accepted as the standard form to be used as a basis for the creation of sigils.

Although the creation of sigils on the kameas is, as far as we know, first documented in Agrippa, the kameas by themselves were being used for magick prior to this. The kameas were inscribed on planetary amulets and talismans made of thin sheets of the planetary metals and used for a wide variety of purposes. A manuscript entitled *The Book of Angels, Rings, Characters & Images of the Planets: attributed to Osbern Bokenham,* dating to the period 1441-45 on planetary magick makes specific reference to use of the kameas in talismanic magick in this manner. This MSS is contained in *Cambridge MSS Dd.xi.45,* between herbal and medical texts, and all written in the same hand.

## Names of Spiritual Creatures

All the names for the spiritual creatures which are converted into sigils on kameas are Hebrew. Each letter of the Hebrew alphabet has an associated numerical value, which is used to help form the unique sigil for the individual creature. By converting the letters of the name into their associated numbers, the sigil can be created by connecting the sequence of numbers formed by this conversion on the appropriate planetary kamea. The sigil for a planetary spiritual creature is always formed by using the appropriate associated planetary kamea as the base, i.e. you would always draw up the sigils for solar spiritual creatures on the solar kamea, etc.

The obvious problem that could arise from this form of sigilisation is that a word could contain letters whose numerical equivalents are larger than the numerical range contained within the kamea which is used as the basis for drawing the sigil on. This is solved by a process of numerical reduction which is known as Aiq Beker or the Qabalah of Nine Chambers. The name Aiq Beker comes from the attribution of the letters to the first two chambers, hence AIQ (Aleph, Yod, Qoph) BKR (Beth, Kaph, Resh).

| 1 | 2 | 3 |
|---|---|---|
| Aleph (A: 1)<br>Yod (I, Y: 10)<br>Qoph (Q: 100) | Beth (B: 2)<br>Kaph (K: 20)<br>Resh (R: 200) | Gimel (G: 3)<br>Lamed (L: 30)<br>Shin (Sh: 300) |
| 4<br>Daleth (D: 4)<br>Mem (M: 40)<br>Tav (Th: 400) | 5<br>Heh (H, E: 5)<br>Nun (N: 50)<br>Final Kaph (K: 500) | 6<br>Vav (V, O, U: 6)<br>Samekh (S: 60)<br>Final Mem (M: 600) |
| 7<br>Zain (Z: 7)<br>Ayin (Aa, O, Ngh: 70)<br>Final Nun (N: 700) | 8<br>Cheth (Ch: 8)<br>Peh (P, Ph: 80)<br>Final Peh (P, Ph: 800) | 9<br>Teth (T: 9)<br>Tzaddi (Tz: 90)<br>Final Tzaddi (Tz: 900) |

If the letter has a higher number attributed to it than exists in the kamea, the number is dropped to the highest number available in the appropriate square of the Aiq Beker table. Thus you can see that the first step in drawing a sigil for a planetary spiritual creature is to work out the numerical sequence for the Hebrew of its name. Hebrew words often have pronunciation marks which add vowels to the English transliteration of the words, but these are not included in the sigils, which are drawn purely from the Hebrew letters which make the word, and the corresponding numbers which they are converted to.

There are certain guidelines which are observed when drawing sigils in this manner, which are as follows:

- ⊕ A circle is usually drawn in the square where the sigil begins and ends. A bar can also be drawn across the starting line in place of a circle to mark the beginning or end of the name.
- ⊕ When a name starts and ends in the same square the sigil can be *"closed"* by joining the end of the final line to the beginning of the first line.
- ⊕ If a name begins with two letters with the same numerical value, a bifurcation like a curvy m may be used, with the line to the next square drawn from the centre of the bifurcation.
- ⊕ When two consecutive letters within a name have the same numerical value, a small loop is drawn, with additional loops for each additional consecutive repetition of the same numerical value.

## Example of Sigil Construction

The principles described previously can be demonstrated by the construction of a sigil for a planetary spiritual creature. Using the Saturnian Planetary Intelligence of Agiel as an example, you can see how the process comes together.

The name Agiel is written in Hebrew as AGIAL, which converts to the numerical sequence of 1(A), 3(G), 10(I), 1(A), 30(L). The Saturn kamea contains the numerical range 1-9, so by Aiq Beker the 10 is reduced to 1 and the 30 is reduced to 3. The sequence of numbers for drawing the sigil then becomes 1, 3, 1, 1, 3.

| | | |
|---|---|---|
| 4 | 9 | 2 |
| 3 | 5 | 7 |
| 8 | 1 | 6 |

The first number is 1 (for A), so a circle is drawn in the centre of the square corresponding to 1 (fig 1). The second number is 3 (for G), so a line is drawn from the circle to the square corresponding to 3 (fig 2). The third number is a 1 (for I, reduced from 10), so a loop is drawn and a line drawn to the square for the number 1 (fig 3). The next letter in the name is A, also with a numeration of 1, so a double loop is drawn to show that there are two consecutive letters attributed to this number (fig 4). Finally the line is drawn to the square with 3 again, (for L, reduced from 30 to 3). As this is the last letter of the sigil, the end is marked with a small circle (fig 5).

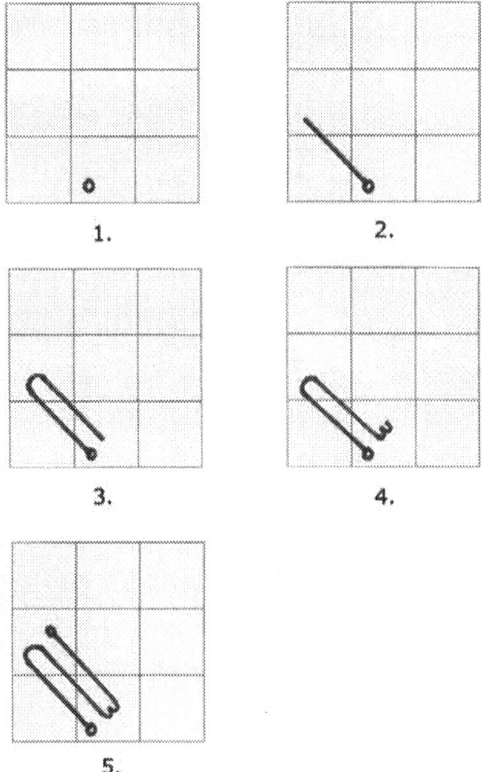

The sigils for the Olympic Spirits are not drawn using this principle, and their origins prior to their appearance in the *Fourth Book of Occult Philosophy* are not known. However it is likely they were Greek in origin and so their creation was obviously not through this technique which uses Hebrew.

## Sigils of Intent

This technique for creating sigils on kameas can also be used to create a sigil of your intent to include on an amulet or talisman. In this case you can apply exactly the same techniques, but keep the word or sequence of words in English and use the table below to convert them into a sequence of numbers to sigillise on the appropriate kamea. It is best to keep the intent as short and precise as possible or your sigil may end up becoming very complicated. A benefit of using this English form of kamea sigilisation is that numbers are always in the 1-9 range and never need to be reduced.

| 1<br>A, J, S | 2<br>B, K, T | 3<br>C, L, U |
|---|---|---|
| 4<br>D, M, V | 5<br>E, N, W | 6<br>F, O, X |
| 7<br>G, P, Y | 8<br>H, Q, Z | 9<br>I, R |

CHAPTER 10

# Amulets & Talismans

When you work with the planets it is to positively increase something in your life that is associated with the planet, or to remove or transform something negative that is associated with the planet. In either case you are looking to improve yourself and your situation, that you may more effectively follow your path through life.

The process of attraction, repulsion or transformation needs to be considered to determine the most effective method of working to achieve your goal, such as an amulet or talisman.

The terms amulet and talisman are often incorrectly used interchangeably. An amulet is a protective charm, used to protect the bearer from specific forces or events. A talisman is used to attract specific energies to enhance a specific aspect of the bearer's situation. So for example, one may own an amulet to protect against lightning strikes or a talisman to attract love.

Amulets and talismans may be carried on you if you need to receive the benefits on an ongoing basis (particularly for amulets), or they may be placed in a safe appropriate place. Thus, e.g. an amulet to protect your car would be stored in the car, whereas a talisman for better communication might be placed near your telephone or computer.

The process of talismanic magick can be summed up in four stages – preparation, creation, purification and consecration. For the purpose of outlining this sequence we are using the term talisman generically, and it could equally be applied to amulets.

## 1. Preparation

The first stage of preparation involves deciding the intent and the components that will be used in the talisman, i.e. the material the talisman is made of and the words and sigils used on the talisman. Once you have decided on your components they need to be acquired. Preparation also involves calculating the planetary hours during which you will perform the purification and consecration. You may also choose to include meditative work with the planet at this stage if you feel you need to develop your understanding of the energies of the planet you will be drawing on.

## 2. Creation

Creation involves the actual construction of the talisman. You draw, etch or engrave the sigils onto your talisman, indicating your intent and the nature of the spiritual creatures or forces you will be drawing upon to empower your talisman. When creating amulets or talismans drawing on planetary energies you will need to decide whether or not you will be doing so on the appropriate metal or alternatively on suitably coloured paper. For most people the decision will be based on considerations of cost and practical skills as metal will by its very nature require special engraving tools and skills if you decide to use it as the basis for your charm.

Additionally, some metals such as gold may incur costs and the sourcing of suitable supplies may also deter all but the very determined when it comes to creating charm made from metal. It is necessary however to emphasise here that charms created on a metal base will by their very nature be more enduring than those created on paper and as such they are recommended for charms which will be used for longer periods of time.

| Planet | No | Metal | Colour |
|---|---|---|---|
| Saturn | 3 | Lead | Black |
| Jupiter | 4 | Tin | Blue |
| Mars | 5 | Brass[26] | Red |
| Sun | 6 | Gold | Gold/Yellow |
| Venus | 7 | Copper | Green |
| Mercury | 8 | Aluminium[27] | Orange |
| Moon | 9 | Silver | Silver/Purple |

In the grimoires the amulets and talismans were usually made on circular disks of metal. However when using paper, the amulet or talisman can alternatively be made with a number of sides equal to the planetary number. If you decide to use white paper or card for your talisman, the ink colour for drawing all the appropriate seals or sigils you decide on should be that of the planetary colour.

Hence a Jupiterian talisman would be on a square piece of blue card. Glyphs usually included on talismans are the astrological sign of the planet, the Divine Name, the name and/or seal of the Archangel, the name and/or sigil of the Planetary Spirit and Intelligence, and any other appropriate symbols desired. The sigils for the Planetary Intelligences and Spirits, and the Hebrew words commonly used on the talismans for the associated planetary spiritual creatures, divine names and concepts are included as Appendix 4 of this work.

---

26 Brass is used for the creation of charms instead of the planetary metal for Mars which is Iron due to the belief that spiritual beings dislike Iron.

27 As Mercury is a liquid a room temperature and extremely toxic it is for obvious reasons unsuitable for creating charms. Aluminium is a light metal used in the construction of aircraft and hence movement between realms (Air & Earth) makes it a suitable metal for use.

## 3. Purification

Purification is the third stage, and is the precursor to the final step of consecration of the talisman. Purification involves ensuring there are no unwanted influences attached to your talisman, effectively making it magickally neutral ready to act as a receptacle and lens for the forces you seek to attract through its action. Purification can also include ritual bathing, ensuring that you too are pure.

## 4. Consecration

The final step of consecration is the activation of the talisman as a focus for the desired planetary energy. Hymns may be included in the consecration ceremony to request assistance, to enhance the effectiveness of both amulets and talismans.

# Consecration Ritual

Having created your amulet or talisman, the following is an outline for the consecration:

## On the altar you need to have:

- ⊕ The Talisman
- ⊕ An appropriately coloured piece of natural material big enough to wrap it in.
- ⊕ Bowl of spring water
- ⊕ Bowl of sea salt
- ⊕ Censer of incense
- ⊕ Red candle

Place your talisman on the piece of coloured fabric on the altar.

## The Procedure:

You may choose to perform the Heptagram Ritual, using the Invoking Heptagram for the planet whose energy you are working with in making the talisman.

Cast a Planetary Circle to perform your consecration within.

## Purification

Before performing your consecration you should purify your talisman to remove all influences, making it effectively a tabula rasa ready to act as your focus for the desired energy.

Take the talisman and pass it through the incense smoke, saying:

*I purify you with the element of Air*

Now pass the talisman (carefully and quickly) through the candle flame, saying:

*I purify you with the element of Fire*

Sprinkle the talisman with a drop of water from the bowl and say:

*I purify you with the element of Water*

Sprinkle a few grains of salt over the talisman and say:

*I purify you with the element of Earth*

The talisman is now purified and ready to be consecrate.

## Consecration

State the intent of the talisman, in a single concise sentence (that you have prepared beforehand), drawing the sigil of the planet in the air over the talisman and visualising it in the appropriate planetary colour. See the sigil shining with an inner brilliance, and then visualise a taut line of force in the appropriate planetary colour from your dominant hand to the sigil. Lower your hand so the sigil descends with it, into the talisman.

Intone in sequence the hierarchy of planetary spiritual creatures for the planet, a number of times equal to the planetary number. Start with the Divine Name, then the Archangel, then the Order of Angels, the name of the Heaven (i.e. the planet), the Planetary Intelligence and finally the Planetary Spirit.

Now raise your arms upwards so they make a V, and declare:

*I will take of the divine spirit [divine name], emanating from the heavens,*
*Focused through the archangel [name] who directs the [order of angels]*
*Manifesting through the power of the heaven of [planet] expressed through*

*[planetary intelligence] and [planetary spirit]*
*I have created this talisman for my glory,*
*I have formed it and I have made it.*

As you make this declaration, feel the planetary force from the planet you are working with descending from the heavens, and collecting in your hands. See the energy there as a glow of the planetary colour surrounding your hands. Bring your hands down simultaneously and place them on the talisman, saying:

*I join this talisman to my life, that the (repeat intent).*
*As above, so below, this is my will, it is so.*

Wrap the talisman in the fabric and put it in a safe place.

Example sequence of the calling of the hierarchy of spiritual creatures for a talisman of Mars:

*Elohim Gibor, Khamael, Seraphim, Mars, Graphiel, Bartzabel (x5)*

Now raise your arms upwards so they make a V, and declare:

*I will take of the divine spirit Elohim Gibor, emanating from the heavens,*
*Focused through the archangel Khamael who directs the Seraphim*
*Manifesting through the power of the heaven of Mars expressed through Graphiel and Bartzabel*
*I have created this talisman for my glory,*
*I have formed it and I have made it.*

CHAPTER 11

# Preparation

For any ceremony there are a number of components to be taken into account before you start. Making sure you have considered all the components ensures your ceremonies are more likely to be successful. These components are:

- ⊕ Intent
- ⊕ Timing
- ⊕ Location
- ⊕ Purification
- ⊕ Circle & Altar
- ⊕ Symbols
- ⊕ Tools
- ⊕ Sequence

## Intent

Any effective ceremony has a very precise intent. You should have formulated this as your first step, as everything else about the ceremony depends on this.

## Timing

The planetary hours and day should have been determined well in advance. You may also wish to check to see if the planet you are working with is undergoing any particular aspects or conjunctions. E.g. you may prefer to not work with a planet when it is retrograde, as this indicates a reversal of energy which is only appropriate for banishing influences.

## Location

Most planetary magick is performed indoors. If you are working indoors, do you have a permanent temple space, or do you need to make a space to work in? In either case the space should be cleaned before the ceremony, and if it is not a permanent temple space, all distractions should be dealt with. This includes turning off all telephones and electrical equipment. If you are working outdoors, double and triple-check that you have everything you will need for your ceremony before leaving the house.

## Purification

An important consideration for magickal work is that everything you use should be purified. Anything you take into a magick circle for ritual work should have been purified. This includes mundane items you might not otherwise consider, such as your pair of glasses if you wear them. Additionally, following purification, if an item has a specific purpose, like a tool or robe, it should also have been consecrated. Consecration involves energising the item in question towards the specific purpose(s) you will be using it for.

Having a ritual bath before a ceremony is always to be recommended, and when you do so you can use appropriately scented bath oils to fragrance your bath and aid in your purification before the ceremony. After drying yourself you should put your robe on rather than clothes, and also any ritual jewellery you may be planning on wearing for the ceremony.

## Circle & Altar

The nature of the work you perform will contribute to your choice of circle. If you are performing invocation or evocation a permanent circle is preferable. For evocation you may also wish to construct a triangle if appropriate. For consecration of talismans or amulets, meditation, or devotion, a subtle circle is appropriate. The altar is usually placed at the centre of the circle. For invocation the receptacle is usually placed on the centre of the altar, and other tools may be placed at the edges of the circle or on the altar as preferred. For work such as the consecration of talismans, the appropriate items all need to be on the altar.

Remember as you are performing a planetary ceremony, you do not need to follow the common model of having elemental tools and representations on your altar. An altar is like a working table, it should only have items there that need to be there. There is no point in having a cup there if you don't need it, for example.

## Symbols

Use of appropriate symbols helps focus the mind on the intent of the ceremony. Using the appropriate planetary colour for your candles and altar cloth, and having an appropriate planetary incense will all help with focusing your mind on the energy you are working with. Your robe may be white or the appropriate planetary colour as desired.

## Tools

Your tools include your robe, magickal weapons, candles, censer & incense, lamen, altar, altar cloth. Lamens should have been made at an appropriate planetary time. All tools should have been purified and consecrated before the ceremony.

## Sequence

Have a clear idea in your head of the *"running order"* of your ceremony. If you are working with planetary hours, be aware of the time constraints and plan accordingly. You can overrun slightly, but the main focus of the ritual should be within the appropriate planetary hour, and any closing up can be done in the subsequent planetary hour. If you are performing conjurations, have copies of anything you plan on reading in clear and large easy-to-read script.

Remember that working in the semi-darkness of candlelight can make it hard to read. If you have memorised the material then a script copy is still useful in case you forget the words, or just to provide you with the confidence that comes from knowing you have planned thoroughly. If you are performing invocation or evocation, have a list of questions prepared beforehand, or it is easy all too easy to get distracted and not cover everything you wanted to.

CHAPTER 12

# The Magick Circle

The magick circle has long been used by magickians as a ritual space. In the modern tradition of Wicca, the magick circle is additionally said to provide a container for the energies raised during a ceremony and the circle itself is often called a *"place between the worlds of man and the Gods"*. This is entirely different to the use of the magick circle in ceremonial magick, where the magician stays in the world of man and effects change, rather than shifting to an in-between space.

A magick circle may be physical and permanent, being marked on the floor, or a board or other suitable material to place on the floor, or it may be a subtle circle created by the magician before performing magickal work. A subtle circle has the benefits of being useable anywhere, and not requiring you to have a permanent temple set up. If you make a permanent circle on a material for placing on the floor, this also does not require a permanent temple, but will take up space wherever you store it.

For work with the Olympic Spirits and Planetary Gods, as well as for the purposes of consecrations and empowerment of talismans and amulets, the subtle magick circle may provide the ideal working conditions. It is however important to be proficient in the creation of the magick circle, prior to starting any ceremonies in which it will be utilized.

For magickal work the altar is usually placed in the centre of the temple. It may be set up in one of two ways, either with any paraphernalia and tools on it, as for consecration of talismans, as is usually the case for work with a subtle magick circle. Alternatively it may be set up with a receptacle for invocation on it, when it is usually kept clear of all other paraphernalia. In such instances items like candles and censers are commonly placed around the edge of the circle, which is normally a permanent circle.

# Planetary Circle (Subtle)

Prepare the space in which you are to perform your ceremony by removing any distractions and cleaning. You will be creating a circle which will be 7 foot in diameter, although you may adapt this to a larger size if you plan on working with others.

## Requirements:

- ⊕ A small bowl containing spring water.
- ⊕ A small bowl of sea salt.
- ⊕ Spirit light (may be lamp with a wick or a candle)

For the creation of the circle you may use a wand or dagger, or your preferred hand. If you use your hand, make the gesture of benediction. This is made by extending the forefinger and big finger, and curling the ring finger and little finger into the palm, with the thumb curled over so it rests on the ring and little fingers.

Before the ceremony commences light the spirit light and the incense. Declare:

*Hekas o hekas este bibeloi*[28]

Add the salt to the bowl of water. As you do so, proclaim:

*Be pure.*

Dip your fingers in the consecrated water. Pick up the bowl of consecrated water and walk around the space, starting in the East, in a

28 Begone all unholiness (Greek).

clockwise circle, sprinkling the consecrated water as you walk. When you have returned to the East, go back to the altar and replace the bowl on the altar and pick up your preferred tool, or make the gesture of benediction. Again go to the East and walk clockwise around your space with your arm outstretched downwards towards the floor and see a circle of white flames being formed at the tip of the weapon or your fingers, and say:

*United the seven deathless powers form the greater unity*
*That unity is my circle, bound in time and space*
*Within is my universe illuminated by the magick of the wandering stars.*
*As above, so below*

When you have returned to the East, return to the centre and place your weapon on the altar, and continue with your ceremony.

# Planetary Circle (Physical)

A permanent magick circle is used for invocation and evocation, and great care should be taken in its construction. The circle is in fact a double circle, with one circle inside the other. The circles are usually painted in white on the ground.

Mark a circle of nine foot diameter, with a concentric circle inside it of eight foot diameter. This will give you an inner circle which is six inches from the outer circle all the way around. In the space between the two circles, at the cardinal points (i.e. East, South, West & North) draw a pentagram, with its point nearest the inner circle, so it appears to face outwards. In the spaces between the pentagrams, write the divine names you are going to use, facing inwards do you can read them from inside the circle. These can be in English or Hebrew depending on your preference, but for convenience we will give them in English here.

Between the North and East write Yahveh, between the East and South write Adonai, between the South and West write Eheia, and between the West and North write Agla.

When you use a permanent circle, it is important to remember that you should use a sword, dagger or wand or other appropriate weapon to trace both the outer and inner circles, to emphasise their integrity as a barrier.

We advocate the use of the banishing pentagram of Active Spirit for the creating of the wards on the circle. This is because it is not an elemental circle, and you are calling spiritual creatures, so Active Spirit is appropriate as the most effective ward to maintain the circle.

Banishing Active Spirit Pentagram

To ensure the integrity and power of your circle, start in the East and walk clockwise around the circle with your weapon pointing towards the outer circle, seeing the marked circle burning with a white fire. Walk a complete circuit back to the East, and then repeat the same for the inner circle.

Now using the dagger or wand, draw the banishing pentagram of Active Spirit in the air over the pentagram marked on the floor in the East, and see it hanging in the air, burning in white flame. Go clockwise around the circle repeating this in the South, West and North.

Moving to the North-East, vibrate the divine name Yahveh, and see the name in the space between the circles in front of you burning with white fire. Move clockwise to the South-East and vibrate the divine name Adonai, again seeing the name on the floor burning with white fire. Continue clockwise to the South-West and vibrate the divine name Eheia, seeing the name on the floor burning with white fire. Continue your circuit to the North-West, and vibrate the divine name Agla, seeing the name on the floor burning with white fire.

The circle is now activated and ready for use for invocation or evocation.

When you have finished your ceremony, as the circle is permanent you obviously do not *"de-cast"* it. Go around the circle anti-clockwise starting in the North, and see each of the flaming white pentagrams in the air descending and superimposing themselves onto the pentagrams beneath them in the space between the circles. This then serves the purpose of further charging these pentagrams with energy as protective wards.

When you have done this, go round the circle a second time anticlockwise, seeing all the white flames in the circles, pentagrams and names being absorbed into the paint of the circle markings.

CHAPTER 13

# The Ritual of the Heptagram

We created this ritual some years ago for use in a magickal group we were facilitating at the time for use in a series of planetary workings. We felt that the Hexagram Ritual of the Hermetic Order of the Golden Dawn which is usually recommended for planetary workings was inadequate for our purposes. Through regular work the ritual has undergone refinements over the years and the version we present here is one we found most effective for solitary or small group workings.

It is best used at the beginning of ceremonies focusing on planetary forces and can also be used as a daily balancing exercise. It can additionally be used at the end of ceremonies to balance and ground excess energy in a harmonious manner.

When performing planetary work it is usual to focus on the energies of a particular planet, for this reason it is necessary to use the appropriate invoking and banishing heptagram in the Ritual of the Heptagram.

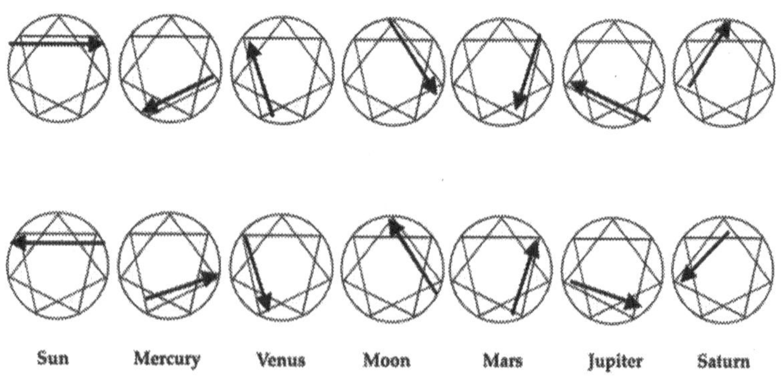


Figure 1 : Invoking & Banishing Planetary Heptagrams

## Instruction:

Stand facing East, with your arms by your sides, palms forward, and say:

*Emmi gas vios kai ouranou asteroentos*[29]

Move your arms upwards into a V with your palms upward and visualise a gold sphere of energy around your heart as you say:

*I stand in the timeless void, my heart burning with the immortal fire*

Move your right arm down in a sweeping movement to your side with the palm facing downward, and visualise a green sphere of energy at your feet, standing on it as you say:

*I draw my power from the earth and the starry heavens*

Move your arms so they are horizontal (crucifix position) with the palms facing forward, and visualise a white sphere of energy at your crown, the bottom of the sphere touching the top of your head as you say:

*I create the holy light that shines in the darkness*

Keeping your arms in the cross position, draw the green energy up the body and the white energy down from the head and see them merge with the gold energy to form an even brighter golden energy at the heart which then spreads and suffuses the aura.

Slowly lower your arms towards your sides again and say:

---

29 "I am a child of earth and starry heaven", the Orphic Oath.

**With Alpha I begin this rite, establishing peace, A*
*With Epsilon, I welcome grace, E*
*With Eta, I cleanse this place, EE*
*With Iota, I focus my will, I*
*With Omicron, I uphold the truth, O*
*With Upsilon, I radiate glory, U*
*With Omega I complete the ordering of chaos, OO*

*In the seven-lettered name I establish the harmony of the heavens*
*A, E, EE, I, O, U, OO*

Move your preferred hand to the starting position for the appropriate planetary Heptagram, and inscribe the heptagram starting at the appropriate point, visualising the lines in the appropriate colour for the planet you are working with. From the top, the points when drawn in front of the body are level with the head (top), 6" above left and right shoulder (upper left and upper right), 6" to the left and right of the body in front of bottom of ribs (middle left and right), in front of left and right hips (bottom left and right).

Raise your arms back into an upwards V shape and say:

*Uniting the seven deathless powers of the universe.*

Cross your arms over your chest and say:

*There is no part of me that is not of the Gods*

*Please note: If you are doing this ritual at the end of your ceremony to balance energies and end your ritual, you should use the appropriate banishing heptagram and say *"With Alpha I end this rite, establishing peace, A"*

**CHAPTER 14**

# Planetary Pyramids

As with the Ritual of the Heptagram, we created the Planetary Pyramids for a magickal group we facilitated a number of years ago, as solitary workings for members to use as preparation for group workings. The idea for these workings was developed out of a similar technique we created for working with the four elements, based on the magickal axiom of *"To Know, To Will, To Dare, To Keep Silent"* which form the basis of successful magickal work. We attributed these four axioms to the four corners of the base of the pyramid, with the fifth axiom of *"To Become"*, which is that of Spirit, attributed to the apex of the pyramid.

The attribution of these powers of the elements in this manner is sometimes called the *"Pyramid of Power"*. Following a discussion of the results we gained from working with the elements in this way and facing a series of planetary workings we decided to experiment with the technique applying the same principle to the seven classical planets.

We attributed a set of correspondences for each of the planetary energies to the bases of the pyramids and devised suitable accompanying visualisations, which we then combined with chanting of names of power to create these powerful and effective workings for solitary use. We have subsequently made small adaptations to enable us to use the same workings in a group environment with great success.

Each Planetary Pyramid working can be used before working with its corresponding planet, as part of the preparation for work or as part of the work itself. It will help you to develop a closer understanding of the energies and nature of each planet in turn, particularly if performed on a regular basis. You may find it useful to record these workings and play them to yourself so you can concentrate entirely on the actual practice.

# The Solar Pyramid

The word used as a mantra in this pyramid is Thelema, which is Greek for *"Will"*. We chose to use it here because Will is particularly associated with the Sun as a Solar attribute, and it is chanted in groups of six repetitions as six is the solar number. The divine name of Sol Invictus (*"Invincible Sun"*) refers to the Roman Sun God, whose name has come to embody the Sun. The colour gold is used throughout the visualisation as the primary solar colour.

The qualities we attributed to the corners of the pyramid are truth, will, beauty and harmony, and their solar nature is emphasised through the accompanying visualisations of the gold feather, sword, solar disk and scales. The feather is associated with truth as the feather of Maat, the Egyptian Goddess of Truth and Harmony, as is the scales. The sword is associated with will throughout magick since the Medieval and Renaissance grimoires, where it is used as a weapon of command to ensure the obedience of spiritual creatures. The Solar disk is by its nature a Solar symbol.

## Solar Pyramid Working

See yourself sitting in a gold square within the circle, whose corners are in the East, South, West and North, touching the edge of the circle. This square symbolises the power of the Sun. In the first corner, in the East, is the first of the four powers of the Sun, that of truth. See the energy of truth as a golden feather in the eastern corner, glowing with an inner vibrancy as it embodies the truth that you live by and the truths of the universe. Concentrate on focusing the energy of truth in the eastern corner of the square.

Truth is not static and changes with the flow of life, so move the truth to the second corner of the square, in the South. Do this with the word Thelema (meaning Will in Greek). Chant Thelema six times to send the energy of truth down the golden edge of the square to the southern corner.

THELEMA (x6)

In the second corner in the South, truth is transformed into the second quality of the Sun, that of will. Truth inspires the will, driving it so that you express your intent on following your true will. Focus on transforming the energy of truth into will at the second corner of the square, in the South, visualising the golden feather changing into a golden sword, point upwards. See the sword flaming with the power of your will.

Now move the power of will to the third corner of the square, in the West. Do this again with the word Thelema, chanting it six times to send the energy of will down the golden edge of the square to the western corner.

THELEMA (x6)

In the third corner in the West, will is transformed into beauty, the third quality of the Sun. Beauty is an expression of will, your will to be as perfect as you can be, the will of life to grow and express itself, of the mind to create beautiful words and images. See the golden sword change into a golden solar disk, radiating golden rays outwards. Focus on gathering the energy of beauty in the third corner of the square, in the West.

Living beauty grows, so move it to the fourth corner of the square, in the North. To do this chant the word Thelema six times to send the energy of beauty down the golden edge of the square to the northern corner.

THELEMA (x6)

Beauty is an expression of inner harmony and outer harmony with the environment. In the North beauty is transformed into the fourth quality of the Sun, that of harmony. Harmony comes from finding balance, and expressing that balance in your thoughts and actions. See the golden solar disk change into a golden pair of scales. Focus on transforming that beauty you have moved here into harmony.

To complete the square move the harmony to the eastern corner. When you are in harmony, you express truth as a natural consequence of your balanced state. To move the harmony to the first corner back in the East chant Thelema six times, to send the energy of harmony down the golden edge of the square to the eastern corner.

THELEMA (x6)

Now you sit within the golden square of the Sun, with its powers of truth, will, beauty and harmony. To use these qualities you must move in time, which means you need to transform the square into three dimensions. Visualise a golden line rising from each of the four corners, to meet in the centre above you, forming a pyramid. As you are completing the pyramid, use the phrase Sol Invictus to express the triumph of life in its myriad forms. So chant Sol Invictus six times to aid the formation of the pyramid as you see the lines rising to the upper central point.

SOL INVICTUS (x6)

Now you sit inside the pyramid of the Sun, in the inner chamber. You are surrounded by the golden energies of beauty and harmony, of truth and will. Draw those golden energies into your heart so that your body and aura are permeated with the golden power of the Sun. Do this until all the energy is absorbed and the pyramid has faded away.

# The Mercurial Pyramid

The word used as a mantra in this pyramid is Azoth. Azoth is a term from alchemy used to describe fluid Mercury as a spiritual essence rather than the physical metal. The word Azoth is formed by taking the Roman letter "A", which is also equated to the Greek *"Alpha"* and Hebrew *"Aleph"*, and then following it with the final letter of each of those alphabets, i.e. the Roman letter "Z", the Greek letter *"Omega"* (O) and the Hebrew letter *"Tav"* (Th). Azoth thus implies the beginning and end. The word Azoth is chanted in groups of eight repetitions as this is the number of Mercury, and likewise the colour orange is used throughout the visualisation as the primary Mercurial colour.

The qualities we attributed to the corners of the pyramid are clarity, knowledge, inspiration and flexibility. These are all qualities associated with Mercury, and this is emphasised by the accompanying visualisations of the orange dagger, quill, lightning bolt and octogram. The dagger represents the clarity of mind that cleaves through superfluity to go straight to the heart of a subject or concept. The quill is indicative of knowledge as the writing implement for recording knowledge. Inspiration is often described as coming *"like a bolt from the blue"*, and the dramatic power and speed of lightning are a good analogy to the flash of inspiration. The octogram or eight-rayed star is Mercurial by its numeration of eight.

## Mercurial Pyramid Working

See yourself sitting in an orange square within the circle, whose corners are in the East, South, West and North, touching the edge of the circle. This square symbolises the power of Mercury. In the first corner, in the East, is the first of the four powers of Mercury, that of clarity. Clarity is the ability to discern the reality of a situation and see things how they are. Concentrate on focusing the energy of clarity in the eastern corner of the square, seeing it as an orange dagger point upwards; the dagger of clarity that cleaves through illusion and deception to show the truth beneath.

Clarity encourages you to grow and move forward, so move the energy of clarity to the second corner of the square, in the South. Do this with the word Azoth. Azoth is the alchemical fluid, the essence of life that permeates all and acts as a catalyst for change and growth towards perfection. Chant Azoth eight times to send the energy of clarity down the orange edge of the square to the southern corner.

AZOTH (x8)

In the second corner in the South, clarity is transformed into the second quality of Mercury, that of knowledge. Knowledge comes from experience and the clarity of thought and deed that bring realisation. Focus on transforming the energy of clarity into knowledge at the second corner of the square, in the South, and see it become an orange feather quill. The quill writes and records knowledge, making it available to all with eyes to see. Think of all the knowledge you have gained in your life, and focus this in the quill in the southern corner

Through gaining knowledge, your horizons widen and you open yourself to growth as you make connections between disparate pieces of knowledge. Now move the energy of knowledge to the third corner of the square, in the West. Do this with the word Azoth, chanting it eight times to send the energy down the orange edge of the square to the western corner.

AZOTH (x8)

In the third corner in the West, knowledge is transformed into inspiration, the third quality of Mercury. Inspiration can come from knowledge you have gained or out of the blue like a bolt of lightning. Focus on gathering the energy of inspiration in the third corner of the square, in the

West, seeing the orange quill change to an orange lightning bolt. Think of times you have been inspired and how you felt, and put the energy that inspires in you into the western corner of the square.

Inspiration also means the intake of breath, moving the energy. To move the energy of inspiration to the northern corner of the square chant the word Azoth eight times to send it down the orange edge of the square to the northern corner.

AZOTH (x8)

With inspiration comes a new flexibility as you realise new possibilities. Flexibility is the fourth quality of Mercury, showing the ability to adapt appropriately as circumstances change. See the orange lightning bolt change into an orange octogram, made of two squares at forty-five degrees to each other. Think of how you are flexible in your life and focus the energy there in the northern corner of the square.

Flexibility implies movement, and to complete the square you must move the energy of flexibility to the eastern corner. To move the flexibility to the first corner back in the East, chant the word Azoth, eight times, to send the energy of flexibility down the orange edge of the square to the eastern corner.

AZOTH (x8)

Now you sit within the orange square of Mercury, with its powers of clarity, knowledge, inspiration and flexibility. To use these qualities you must move in time, which means you need to transform the square into three dimensions. Visualise an orange line rising from each of the four corners, to meet in the centre above you, forming a pyramid. As you are completing the pyramid, use the name Azoth, chanting it eight times to aid the formation of the pyramid as you see the lines rising to the upper central point.

AZOTH (x8)

Now you sit inside the pyramid of Mercury, in the inner chamber. Draw the orange Mercurial energy into your heart, filling your body and aura with the powers of clarity, knowledge, inspiration and flexibility, absorbing all the energy until the pyramid has faded away.

# The Venusian Pyramid

Unlike the previous pyramid meditations, a number of words are used in this meditation. The four words used as mantras for sending the energy around the base of the pyramid are Philia, Agapé, Eros, and Storge. These words all emphasise the concept of love, which is particularly associated with Venus. The four words are all Greek, being friendship (Philia), spiritual or unconditional love (Agapé), physical or sexual love (Eros) and familial love (Storge). The word used as a mantra to visualise the upward edges which extend the pyramid into three dimensions is Elohim, which is the Hebrew Divine Name associated with Venus as the sphere of Netzach on the Tree of Life. Elohim means *"Gods"*, and emphasises multiplicity of the divine manifestations in a similar way to the expression of different manifestations of love. The words are chanted in groups of seven repetitions as this is the number of Venus, and emerald green is used as the colour for the same reason of correspondence with Venus.

The qualities we attributed to the corners of the pyramid are liberty, light, life and love. These are all qualities associated with radiation of positive concepts which are both life-affirming and life-enhancing. Liberty is a quality that can be taken for granted by those who have it, but consider the implications. Liberty means you can go where you want and are free to express your opinions and have rights. Light is a requisite for most life, love brings its own benefits and pleasures, and life is (or should be) its own reward. The accompanying visualisations for these concepts are less *"sharp"* than in the other meditations as the concepts are harder in some respects to symbolise. Glow and brilliance are both types of light. The Hebrew word for Venus is *"Nogah"*, which also means *"glow"*, and brilliance indicates the highest form of light. The pulsating brilliance visualisation associated with love is symbolic of the beating of the heart, the organ associated with love, and this visualisation is maintained for life as it is also appropriate there.

## The Venus Pyramid Working

See yourself sitting in an emerald green square within the circle, whose corners are in the East, South, West and North, touching the edge of the circle. This square symbolises the power of Venus. In the first corner, in the East, is the first of the four powers of Venus, that of liberty. Liberty is freedom, freedom of deed and thought, freedom of movement. Like air, liberty is invisible and all around you. Think of the winds and how they blow free, unrestricted. Concentrate on focusing the energy of liberty in the eastern corner of the square. See it as a transparent green glow in the eastern corner of the square.

Liberty cannot be contained, so move the liberty to the second corner of the square, in the South. Do this with the word Philia, representing friendship, for true friendship is liberating and helps you grow. Chant Philia seven times to send the energy of liberty down the green edge of the square to the southern corner.

PHILIA (x7)

In the second corner in the South, liberty is transformed into the second quality of Venus, that of light. The light of the morning and evening star, the light of illumination which shines on the path of the mysteries, the light of the divine spark within you. Focus on transforming the energy of liberty into light at the second corner of the square, in the South, and see it become a brilliant emerald green light.

Light illuminates wherever it travels, so now move the light to the third corner of the square, in the West. Do this with the word Agapé, representing spiritual love, the pure unconditional love of self, love of others, and love of life that is illuminated with inner harmony. Chant Agapé seven times to send the emerald green light down the green edge of the square to the western corner.

AGAPÉ (x7)

In the third corner in the West, light is transformed into love, the third quality of Venus. Love is expressed through thoughts and actions, and the perfect love you feel for your family and friends. Love of yourself, love of others, love of life. Love is the greatest power in the universe. Focus on gathering the energy of love in the third corner of the square, in the West. See the radiant green emerald light, pulsing in time with your heartbeat.

Love moves and flows, so move it to the fourth corner of the square, in the North. To do this chant the word Eros, physical love. Love is expressed in union with others, and when life comes forth from this love, it is truly blessed. Chant Eros seven times to send the energy of love down the green edge of the square to the northern corner.

EROS (x7)

With love comes life, for love permeates the universe engendering life and love of life, the fourth quality of Venus, and one associated with family. You experience life, its own reward, as you seek to realise your divine potential and become the best you can be. See the energy of life, still pulsing in time with your heart, emerald green and brilliant.

To complete the square you must move the life to the eastern corner. As you move through life, you strive for liberty, to be yourself and do what you need to do to fulfil your path. To move the life to the first corner back in the East chant the word Storge, familial love, seven times, to send the energy of life down the green edge of the square to the eastern corner.

STORGE (x7)

Now you sit within the green square of Venus, with its powers of life, light, love and liberty. To use these qualities you must move in time, which means you need to transform the square into three dimensions. Visualise a green line rising from each of the four corners, to meet in the centre above you, forming a pyramid. As you are completing the pyramid, use the name Elohim, which means Gods, to celebrate the gods who act through you, empowering and inspiring you on your path. So chant Elohim seven times to aid the formation of the pyramid as you see the lines rising to the upper central point.

ELOHIM (x7)

Now you sit inside the pyramid of Venus, in the inner chamber. And herein is a mystery, for the inner chamber is the name of Yah, the first two letters of the fourfold name, combining the feminine and masculine in union, as you do yourself, within the pyramid of Venus. Draw the green Venusian energy into your heart, filling your body and aura with the powers of light, life, love and liberty, absorbing all the energy until the pyramid has faded away.

# The Lunar Pyramid

The word we chose to use as a mantra for this pyramid is Luna, which means *"Moon"* and is also the name of the Lunar Goddess. The word is chanted in groups of nine repetitions as the Lunar number, and silver is used as the colour for the visualisation as the main Lunar colour.

The qualities we attributed to the corners of this pyramid are creativity, imagination, dreams and the unconscious. All of these qualities are directly associated with the Moon, and we chose to represent them with the phases of the Moon as appropriate to their nature, and also demonstrating the cyclic nature of the Moon. Hence the four accompanying visualisations are the New Moon, Half Moon, Full Moon and Dark Moon.

## Lunar Pyramid Working

See yourself sitting in a silver square within the circle, whose corners are in the East, South, West and North, touching the edge of the circle. This square symbolises the power of the Moon. In the first corner, in the East, is the first of the four powers of the Moon, that of creativity. Creativity is the root of our growth, the undercurrent that flows through our lives inspiring us to try new things. Concentrate on focusing the energy of creativity in the eastern corner of the square, seeing it as a New Moon.

The New Moon represents the beginning of a cycle, as creativity is often the beginning of the process of realisation and manifestation. Creativity encourages you to do things and spring into action, so move the energy of creativity to the second corner of the square, in the South. Do this with the word Luna. Chant Luna nine times to send the energy of creativity down the silver edge of the square to the southern corner.

LUNA (x9)

In the second corner in the South, creativity is transformed into the second quality of the Moon, that of imagination. Imagination is the wings that let your mind fly free, exploring possibilities and harnessing the power of the unconscious. Focus on transforming the energy of creativity into imagination at the second corner of the square, in the South, and see the New Moon become a half Moon. The half Moon is light and dark in balance, emphasising the union of the conscious and unconscious mind. Focus this in the half Moon in the southern corner

Through the imagination you can give form to your dreams, making them more tangible. Now move the energy of creativity to the third corner of the square, in the West. Do this with the word Luna, chanting it nine times to send the energy down the silver edge of the square to the western corner.

LUNA (x9)

In the third corner in the West, imagination is transformed into dreams, the third quality of the Moon. Dreams can be the language of the unconscious bubbling up into your conscious mind, and dreams can be the goals you set yourself to achieve. Both have a rich and full value to making you move forward on your path. Focus on gathering the energy of your dreams in the third corner of the square, in the West, seeing the half Moon change to a Full Moon.

Dreams cause us to assess and make changes, so recognising this, move the energy of dreams to the northern corner of the square, by chanting the word Luna nine times to send it down the silver edge of the square to the northern corner.

LUNA (x9)

The dreams that come when you sleep are the symbolic messages and language of your unconscious, the unseen yet vital part of your life that helps you develop by listening to yourself. The unconscious, the store of all your knowledge and experience, is the fourth power of the Moon. See the Full Moon darken and become a dark moon, representing the hidden quality of your unconscious, below the surface like the undercurrents of the oceans that the Moon pulls.

Your unconscious is pulled by the tides of your actions, and so to complete the square you must move the energy of the unconscious to the eastern corner. To move the energy of the unconscious to the first corner back in the east chant the word Luna, nine times, to send the energy down the silver edge of the square to the eastern corner.

LUNA (x9)

Now you sit within the silver square of the Moon, with its powers of creativity, imagination, dreams and the unconscious. To use these qualities you must move in time, which means you need to transform the square into three dimensions. Visualise a silver line rising from each of the four corners, to meet in the centre above you, forming a pyramid. As you are completing the pyramid, use the name Luna, chanting it nine times to aid the formation of the pyramid as you see the lines rising to the upper central point.

LUNA (x9)

Now you sit inside the pyramid of the Moon, in the inner chamber. Draw the silver Lunar energy into your heart, filling your body and aura with the powers of creativity, imagination, dreams and the unconscious absorbing all the energy until the pyramid has faded away.

# The Martial Pyramid

The word we chose to use as a mantra for this pyramid is the Hebrew word Madim, which is used in Qabalah, and literally means *"Mars"* and can also mean *"redness"* (and has five letters). It is chanted in groups of five repetitions as five is the Martial number, and scarlet is used in the visualisations as the Martial colour.

The qualities we attributed to the corners of this pyramid are assertiveness, power, courage and strength. All of these qualities are associated with the dynamic and energetic nature of Mars. Assertiveness is represented by a hand, as the raised or outstretched hand is often symbolic of standing firm and being assertive. The pentagram for power is a Martial symbol as the five-pointed star, and also implies a balance of forces, which is needed to establish power. The heart for courage is a classical attribution, and the bulls' horns for strength symbolise the sustained strength seen in beasts of burden, and also their potency.

## The Mars Pyramid Working

See yourself sitting in a scarlet red square within the circle, whose corners are in the East, South, West and North, touching the edge of the circle. This square symbolises the power of Mars. In the first corner, in the East, is the first of the four powers of Mars, that of assertiveness. See the energy of assertiveness as a red hand, fingers together, facing you, embodying your power to be firm and stand for what you believe in, and be able to say no. Concentrate on focusing the energy of assertiveness in the eastern corner of the square.

Assertiveness is an action, so move the energy of assertiveness to the second corner of the square, in the South. Do this with the word Madim. Chant Madim five times to send the energy of assertiveness down the scarlet edge of the square to the southern corner.

MADIM (x5)

In the second corner in the South, assertiveness is transformed into the second quality of Mars, that of power. Power is energy in motion, driving your focus so that you express your intent. Focus on transforming the energy of assertiveness into power at the second corner of the square, in the South, visualising the red hand changing into a red pentagram, point upwards. See the pentagram flaming scarlet with the power of your will.

Now move the power to the third corner of the square, in the West. Do this again with the word Madim, chanting it five times to send the power down the scarlet edge of the square to the western corner.

MADIM (x5)

In the third corner in the West, power is transformed into courage, the third quality of Mars. Courage is an expression of assertiveness, inner strength to act on your principles and stand up for what you believe, to do what is right. See the red pentagram change into a red heart, beating in time with your own. Focus on gathering the energy of courage in the third corner of the square, in the West.

Courage brings action, so move it to the fourth corner of the square, in the North. To do this chant the word Madim five times to send the energy of courage down the scarlet edge of the square to the northern corner.

MADIM (x5)

Courage requires strength, strength of will and emotional strength. In the North, courage is transformed into the fourth quality of Mars that of strength. Strength is a result of being true to yourself, and developing your qualities to make you a stronger person. See the red heart change into a red pair of bull horns pointing upwards. Focus on transforming that courage you have moved here into strength, and recognise your own strengths.

To complete the square move the energy of strength to the eastern corner. To move the energy of strength to the first corner back in the east chant Madim five times, to send the energy of strength down the scarlet edge of the square to the eastern corner.

MADIM (x5)

Now you sit within the red square of Mars with its powers of assertiveness, power, courage and strength. To use these qualities you must move in time, which means you need to transform the square into three dimensions. Visualise a scarlet line rising from each of the four corners, to meet in the centre above you, forming a pyramid. As you are completing the pyramid, use the phrase Madim, chanting it five times to aid the formation of the pyramid as you see the lines rising to the upper central point.

MADIM (x5)

Now you sit inside the pyramid of Mars in the inner chamber. You are surrounded by the scarlet energies of assertiveness and power, of courage and strength. Draw those scarlet energies into your heart so that your body and aura are permeated with the fiery power of Mars. Do this until all the energy is absorbed and the pyramid has faded away.

# The Jupiterian Pyramid

We chose the Tetragrammaton or fourfold name for its association with Jupiter both through the number of letters and its use in Qabalah. It is created through the construction of the pyramid one additional letter per side of the pyramid, and then pronounced in its usual form when the pyramid is extended into three dimensions. The cumulative names are pronounced in groups of four repetitions as the Jupiterian number, and blue is used as the Jupiterian colour for the visualisations.

The qualities we attributed to the corners of this pyramid are luck, compassion, love and trust. These are all traditionally associated with Jupiter, and have appropriate Jupiterian symbols connected with them. The horseshoe is classically connected with luck, and the blue lotus is traditionally associated with compassion. The blue rose is connected with perfection in alchemy, and is thus a good symbol of love in its highest form. The handshake symbolises trust through agreement and friendship.

## Jupiterian Pyramid Working

See yourself sitting in a blue square within the circle, whose corners are in the East, South, West and North, touching the edge of the circle. This square symbolises the power of Jupiter. In the first corner, in the East, is the first of the four powers of Jupiter, that of luck. Like air, luck is invisible and all around you. Think of things like the four-leafed clover and horseshoe, believed to bring luck, and the energy of luck that permeates them. Concentrate on focusing the energy of luck in the eastern corner of the square as a blue horseshoe pointing upwards.

Luck is not static, so move the luck to the second corner of the square, in the South. Do this with the letter Yod, the first letter of the fourfold name. Chant Yod four times to send the energy of luck down the blue edge of the square to the southern corner.

YOD (x4)

In the second corner in the South, luck is transformed into the second quality of Jupiter, that of compassion. When you have luck you feel benevolent and well disposed to the world, and you demonstrate compassion, by sharing your good luck with others. Compassion is one of the greatest magickal qualities, for it is an expression of unconditional love, for others, for life. Focus on transforming the energy of luck into compassion at the second corner of the square, in the South, visualising the energy of compassion as a blue lotus flower. Now move the compassion to the third corner of the square, in the West. Do this with the letters Yod Heh, the first and second letters of the fourfold name. Chant Yod Heh four times to send the energy of compassion down the blue edge of the square to the western corner.

YOD HEH (x4)

In the third corner in the West, compassion is transformed into love, the third quality of Jupiter. Love is expressed through compassion, and the perfect love you feel for your close friends and family. Love of yourself, love of others, love of life. Love is the greatest power in the universe. Focus on gathering the energy of love in the third corner of the square, in the west, and transform the blue lotus of compassion into a blue rose.

Love moves and flows, so move it to the fourth corner of the square, in the North. To do this chant the three letters Yod Heh Vav, the first three letters of the fourfold name. Chant Yod Heh Vav four times to send the energy of love down the blue edge of the square to the northern corner.

YOD HEH VAV (x4)

With perfect love comes perfect trust, and trust is the fourth quality of Jupiter. You trust in yourself and in those within your life. Focus on transforming that love you have moved here to the North into trust, changing the blue rose into a blue pair of hands in a handshake.

To complete the square move the trust to the eastern corner. When you trust yourself and the gods and the universe, you can experience luck, and sometimes you have to rely on trust alone. To move the trust to the first corner back in the East chant the four letters Yod Heh Vav Heh, the fourfold name, four times, to send the energy of trust down the blue edge of the square to the eastern corner.

YOD HEH VAV HEH (x4)

Now you sit within the blue square of Jupiter, with its powers of luck, compassion, love and trust. To use these qualities you must move in time, which means you need to transform the square into three dimensions. Visualise a line rising from each of the four corners, to meet in the centre above you, forming a pyramid. As you are completing the pyramid, use the fourfold name in its entirety, rather than as its component letters. So chant YAHVEH four times to aid the formation of the pyramid as you see the lines rising to the upper central point.

YAHVEH (x4)

Now you sit inside the pyramid of Jupiter, in the inner chamber. And herein is a mystery, for the inner chamber is the name of Yah, the first two letters of the fourfold name, combining the feminine and masculine in union. You are united, a complete being containing the divine spark, within the pyramid of Jupiter. Draw the blue energy of Jupiter into your heart, the powers of luck, compassion, love and trust. Keep drawing them in and filling your aura and body with them until the pyramid has faded away.

# The Saturnian Pyramid

The word we chose to use as a mantra for this pyramid is IAO, the Gnostic divine name which is also a contraction of the Hebrew divine name of Tetragrammaton. IAO symbolises a range of meanings, including the great divine, and also has three letters, the number of Saturn. It is chanted in groups of three repetitions as the Saturnian number, and black is used as the colour of all the visualisations as the Saturnian colour.

The qualities we attributed to the corners of this pyramid are awareness, transformation, efficiency and stillness. Saturn is often maligned and its positive qualities ignored, but they are important qualities. Awareness is represented by an eye, symbolising the ability to see and thus be aware of your surroundings. The black sun is an alchemical symbol of transformation within the solidity of the earth, which we felt was appropriate here as a symbol of the transforming power of Saturn. The upward pointing hand as a symbol of efficiency reflects the ability of the hand to grip and manipulate objects. The obsidian ball for stillness represents the passivity associated with skrying and also the Saturnian quality of time, seeing visions and the future in an obsidian ball being a popular magickal act for many centuries.

## Saturnian Pyramid Working

See yourself sitting in a black square within the circle, whose corners are in the East, South, West and North, touching the edge of the circle. This square symbolises the power of Saturn. In the first corner, in the East, is the first of the four powers of Saturn, that of awareness. See the energy of awareness as a black eye, like the Eye of Horus in the eastern corner, open and taking all in with its awareness. Concentrate on focusing the energy of awareness in the eastern corner of the square; awareness of yourself, your thoughts, deeds and body, and your environment.

Awareness changes with time, so move the awareness to the second corner of the square, in the South. Do this with the word IAO chanted three times to send the energy of awareness down the black edge of the square to the southern corner.

IAO (x3)

In the second corner in the South, awareness is changed into the second quality of Saturn, that of transformation. Transformation of your self as you pursue your path, improving your mind, your actions, your health, becoming the best you can be. Focus on the energy of transformation at the second corner of the square, in the South, visualising a black solar disk, the black sun of alchemy that symbolises transformation.

Now move the power of transformation to the third corner of the square, in the West. Do this again with the word IAO, chanting it three times to send the energy of transformation down the black edge of the square to the western corner.

IAO (x3)

In the third corner in the West, transformation is changed into efficiency, the third quality of Saturn. Efficiency is an expression of transformation, becoming more effective at doing things in the best and simplest way possible. See the black sun change into an ebony black hand with its fingers pointing upwards. Focus on gathering the energy of efficiency in the third corner of the square, in the West.

Efficiency brings change, so move it to the fourth corner of the square, in the north. To do this chant the word IAO three times to send the energy of efficiency down the black edge of the square to the northern corner.

IAO (x3)

Efficiency is an expression of inner harmony and outer action. In the North efficiency is transformed into the fourth quality of Saturn, that of stillness. Inner stillness when you find the silence within, and outer stillness when your environment is in balance. See the ebony black hand change into a black obsidian sphere. Focus on transforming that efficiency you have moved here into stillness.

Stillness can come in action as well as repose, so to complete the square move the stillness to the eastern corner. To move the stillness to the first corner back in the east chant IAO three times, to send the energy of stillness down the black edge of the square to the eastern corner.

IAO (x3)

Now you sit within the black square of Saturn, with its powers of awareness, transformation, efficiency and stillness. To use these qualities you must move in time, which means you need to transform the square into three dimensions. Visualise a black line rising from each of the four corners, to meet in the centre above you, forming a pyramid. As you are completing the pyramid, chant IAO three times to aid the formation of the pyramid as you see the lines rising to the upper central point.

IAO (x3)

Now you sit inside the pyramid of Saturn, in the inner chamber. You are surrounded by the energies of awareness, transformation, stillness and efficiency. The pyramid of Saturn is the highest of the pyramids, reflecting the energy of the City of Pyramids, where force first becomes form. Draw those dark energies into your heart so that your body and aura are permeated with the black power of Saturn. Do this until all the energy is absorbed and the pyramid has faded away.

**CHAPTER 15**

# The Trans-Saturnian Planets

Although the focus of this work is the seven Classical Planets, for the sake of completion we have included information on the so-called trans-Saturnian planets of Uranus, Neptune and Pluto. Although Pluto has now been declared a planetoid rather than a planet (a matter of size), it has been used in magick since its discovery in 1930 and is included here for this reason.

The basic information on the planets, plus invocations to the associated classical gods are included, providing sufficient information should you wish to apply the principles and techniques used elsewhere in the book to create rituals with these planets.

# Uranus

| | |
|---|---|
| **Numbers** | 11, 121 |
| **Colour** | Purple |
| **Rules** | Aquarius |
| **Metal** | Titanium |
| **Day of the Week** | Wednesday |
| **Element** | Air |
| **Direction** | Above |
| **Concepts** | Heavens, Magick, Reality, Revolution, Transformation |
| **Animals** | Bee, Butterfly, Camel, Fox, Ibis, Jackal, Jaguar, Moth, Khephra, Spider, Vulture, Wolf |
| **Crystals** | Amethyst, Labradorite, Rhodolite, Sphene, Tourmaline |
| **Plants** | Morning Glory |
| **Scents** | Ambergris, Garlic |
| **Symbols** | Web |
| **Tools** | Bell, Cloak, Cords |
| **Gods** | Ouranos, Uranus |

## The Uranian God

Uranus is the Roman god who was the father of Saturn, whose name means *"sky"* or *"heaven"*. He was castrated by his son Saturn with a flint or diamond sickle, who then threw his genitals into the sea. Some versions of the myth have Venus being born from the blood from his genitals and foam of the sea. Uranus was equated to the Greek Ouranos, and his associated myth. The magickal image of Uranus is of a strong but elderly bearded man. Uranus is the least often anthropomorphised of the gods, hence the lesser amount of detail in his magickal image.

## Hymn to Uranus

Lord of heaven whose body never respite knows
Father of all from whom the world arose
The stars within you the source and end of all
Forever shining down on this earthly ball
You are the abode of gods and your power surrounds
This fertile world with ever enduring bounds
Constellations rise and fall within your eyes
As you hold us within the eternal skies
Ethereal and earthly of all-containing frame
Azure and full of life no power can tame
All-seeing heaven and progenitor of time
Blessed Uranus forever you shine
Propitious to my rites ever incline
And crown my wishes with a life divine

## The Sigil of Uranus

The sigil of Uranus is a circle surmounted by an equal-armed cross, with two crescents facing outwards, one on each of the ends of the horizontal line of the cross. The elemental balance of the cross is radiated outwards as change (the two crescents) and dominates spirit (circle), indicating the manifestation and radiation of ideas into reality, which fits with the revolutionary nature of Uranus.

# Neptune

| | |
|---|---|
| **Numbers** | 2 |
| **Colour** | Grey |
| **Rules** | Pisces |
| **Metal** | Tungsten |
| **Day of the Week** | Monday |
| **Element** | Water |
| **Direction** | Seaward |
| **Concepts** | Inner Space, Sea, Tides, Unknown |
| **Animals** | Albatross, Dolphin, Fish, Heron, Horse, Octopus, Sea Horse, Sea-Urchin, Shark, Whale, Capricorn Goat, Kelpi, Kraken, Meliai, Mer-Creatures, Sea Serpents, Sirens |
| **Crystals** | Bezoar, Crabs Eye, Pearl, Rutile, Rutile Quartz |
| **Plants** | Anemone, Ash, Dulse & other Seaweeds, Orchid, Plankton |
| **Scents** | Musk |
| **Symbols** | Trident |
| **Tools** | Shells |
| **Gods** | Neptune, Poseidon |

## The Neptunian God

Neptune is the Roman god of the sea, horses and earthquakes, who was a son of Saturn and brother to Jupiter and Pluto. His name may come from the root *"nebh"* meaning *"moisture"*, giving a meaning of *"God of Moisture"*. He was originally associated with springs and streams prior to his identification with the Greek sea god Poseidon.

The magickal image of Neptune is a crowned and bearded strong man bearing a trident in one hand, in a chariot pulled by two seahorses or sea-goats.

## Hymn to Neptune

Hear me Neptune ruler of the sea profound
Whose liquid grasp defines the solid ground
Who in the deepest realms of the sea
Reign unchallenged in your mighty supremacy
You hold the brazen trident in your hand
And drive your awesome waves onto the land
From your dark locks the briny waters glide
As in your chariot across the foam you ride
Earth shaker whom the trembling waves obey
And to whom the watery denizens do pray
Your voice is heard throughout the deep
The waters movements to your will do keep
Bring gentle peace and prosperous health beside
And pour abundance in your endless tide

## The Sigil of Neptune

The sigil of Neptune is an equal-armed cross surmounted by a crescent horns up, bisected by the upper vertical arm of the cross, forming the trident. The equal-armed cross of elemental balance is influenced by the tidal nature of the Moon, which is also indicated by the symbolism of the sea (crescent) and the seabed and coast (cross).

# Pluto

| | |
|---|---|
| **Numbers** | 1 |
| **Colour** | White |
| **Rules** | Scorpio |
| **Metal** | Platinum |
| **Day of the Week** | Saturday |
| **Element** | Earth |
| **Direction** | Below |
| **Concepts** | Invisibility, Treasure, Underworld |
| **Animals** | Crane, Crayfish, Dog, Dragon, Swan, Wolf |
| **Crystals** | Diamond, Fluorite, Zircon |
| **Plants** | Ebony, Fungi |
| **Scents** | Almond, Amaranth |
| **Symbols** | Crown |
| **Tools** | Helmet, Hood, Keys, Lamp |
| **Gods** | Hades, Pluto |

## The Plutonian God

Pluto is the Roman god of the underworld and wealth. His name comes from the Latin *"pluton"*, which is derived from the Greek word *"ploutos"* meaning *"wealth"*. He was another son of Saturn, and thus brother to Jupiter and Neptune. In later times he was equated with the Greek underworld god Hades, and the whole *"Abduction of Persephone"* myth associated with him, with Persephone becoming Proserpina.

The magickal image of Pluto is a dark stern man in a black cloak. He may wear a helmet (the helmet of invisibility) and may bear a bag of coins or jewels in one hand.

## Hymn to Pluto

Magnanimous Pluto whose realms profound
Are hidden beneath the firm and solid ground
Wrapped forever in the depths of night
Remote from strife and the sun's bright light
The earth's keys to thee great king belong
The secret gates unlocking deep and strong
Your throne is set in Hades' dismal plains
Where not knowing rest your darkness reigns
O mighty king whose decisions dread
The fate determines of the dead
Death's power ruling in sacred night
Dispensing justice with mercy and might
Propitious to my works incline
Rejoicing come for holy rites are thine

## The Sigil of Pluto

The sigil of Pluto is an equal-armed cross surmounted by a crescent horns up, and above the crescent a circle which is partially surrounded by the crescent. The cross being at the bottom under the crescent and circle hints at the underworld nature of Pluto, with perfection (circle) and the tides of time (crescent) both above the earth (cross) at the bottom, showing all must eventually journey into the underworld.

CHAPTER 16

# Angle Webs

David created this technique in 1987, after considering sigilisation techniques and developing ideas for creating a sigil that captures a moment in time to draw on the energy of that particular time to power a talisman. The Angle Web sigil is created by superimposing a symbolic macrocosmic / microcosmic map (the Qabalistic Tree of Life, representing both the universe and man) onto an astrological map of a given moment in time.

The sigil acts as a focus for a given moment in space and time, enabling you to tap into the energy of a particular important event such as an eclipse, significant astrological conjunction, historical event, etc. All the planetary relationships at that time are recreated by the sigil, emphasising the positions and powers of the planets at the moment in time.

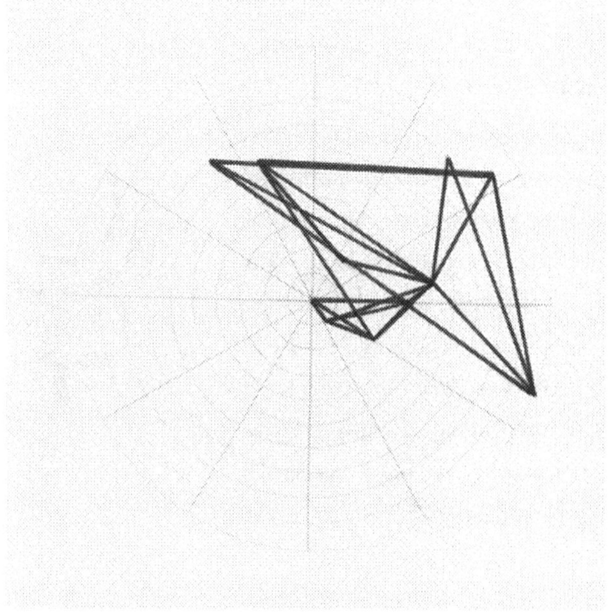

Example Angleweb for midnight of the Millenium in London, UK

Software to draw up natal charts for any moment at any place is easily available freely online now, and can be used to provide you with the basic information you need to construct an angle web. By placing the angle web on the reverse side of a talisman, you are adding another source of energy to your talisman, to empower it for effective results.

## Instruction:

- ⊕ Draw 10 concentric circles at equal intervals outwards from a central point.
- ⊕ Very lightly draw 12 equidistant radii to the outer circle, dividing all the circles into 12 equal segments. These divisions represent the astrological signs, so start with Aries at the top (in the North position), and the other signs follow round in an anti-clockwise direction.
- ⊕ The centre of the circle represents the planet Earth (because this is Malkuth qabalistically, and because that is where we are, so that is where we want to focus the energy!). Moving out from the centre the planets are placed on the circumferences of the respective circles relative to their mean distance from Earth, and based on their astrological position at the time the sigil is being drawn for.
- ⊕ In order out from the centre, the planets follow this sequence - Moon, Mars, Venus, Mercury, Sun, Jupiter, Saturn, Uranus, Neptune, Pluto. Thus if the sign of Aries began at the top of the page, and the Moon was 28° Taurus, the Moon would be located at approximately the *10 o clock* position on the rim of the first circle.
- ⊕ When all the planets have been marked in their respective places on their respective circles, each planet should be joined to the other planets it would be connected to on the Tree of Life, using the standard attributions. Hence the centre, Earth (Malkuth),

would be joined to the Moon (Yesod) on the first circle, Venus (Netzach) on the third circle and Mercury (Hod) on the fourth circle. This method uses the classic attribution of Saturn to Binah on the Tree of Life, with Uranus to Daath, Neptune to Chokmah and Pluto to Kether.

The table that follows shows all the connections that need to be made between the points representing the planets on the concentric circles.

| Planet | Position | Connects to |
|---|---|---|
| Earth | Centre | Moon, Mercury, Venus |
| Moon | First circle | Mercury, Venus, Sun |
| Mars | Second circle | Jupiter, Saturn |
| Venus | Third circle | Sun, Jupiter |
| Mercury | Fourth circle | Venus, Sun, Mars |
| Sun | Fifth circle | Mars, Jupiter, Saturn, Uranus, Neptune, Pluto |
| Jupiter | Sixth circle | Neptune |
| Saturn | Seventh circle | Neptune, Pluto |
| Uranus | Eight circle | Pluto |
| Neptune | Ninth circle | Pluto |
| Pluto | Tenth circle | - |

Pluto does not have any connections as it is the top of the Tree of Life and therefore has already had all its connecting paths drawn in.

The Angle Web should be drawn in an appropriate planetary colour for the nature of your talisman. After all the planets have been connected, the Angle Web is constructed, and ready for adding to your talisman to empower it when you consecrate the talisman.

# APPENDIX

APPENDIX 1

# Inter-Planetary Relationships

It is interesting to note from the grimoires that the planets were not all perceived as having positive relationships. A summary of the planetary relationships taken from the work of Agrippa is given in the following table.

| Relationship | Sun | Mercury | Venus | Moon | Mars | Jupiter | Saturn |
|---|---|---|---|---|---|---|---|
| **Sun towards** | | Enemy | Love | Enemy | Enemy | Love | Friend |
| **Mercury towards** | Enemy | | Friend | Enemy | Enemy | Friend | Friend |
| **Venus towards** | Love | Love | | Love | Love | Love | Enemy |
| **Moon towards** | Enemy | Enemy | Friend | | Enemy | Friend | Friend |
| **Mars towards** | Enemy | Enemy | Love | Enemy | | Enemy | Enemy |
| **Jupiter towards** | Friend | Friend | Friend | Friend | Enemy | | Friend |
| **Saturn towards** | Friend | Friend | Enemy | Friend | Enemy | Friend | |

## APPENDIX 2

# The Kameas

### Saturn

| | | |
|---|---|---|
| 4 | 9 | 2 |
| 3 | 5 | 7 |
| 8 | 1 | 6 |

*Number of Squares = 9; Row/Column total = 15; Square total = 45*

### Jupiter

| | | | |
|---|---|---|---|
| 4 | 14 | 15 | 1 |
| 9 | 7 | 6 | 12 |
| 5 | 11 | 10 | 8 |
| 16 | 2 | 3 | 13 |

*Number of Squares = 16; Row/Column total = 34; Square total = 136*

### Mars

| | | | | |
|---|---|---|---|---|
| 11 | 24 | 7 | 20 | 3 |
| 4 | 12 | 25 | 8 | 16 |
| 17 | 5 | 13 | 21 | 9 |
| 10 | 18 | 1 | 14 | 22 |
| 23 | 6 | 19 | 2 | 15 |

*Number of Squares = 25; Row/Column total = 65; Square total = 325*

**Sun**

| | | | | | |
|---|---|---|---|---|---|
| 6 | 32 | 3 | 34 | 35 | 1 |
| 7 | 11 | 27 | 28 | 8 | 30 |
| 19 | 14 | 16 | 15 | 23 | 24 |
| 18 | 20 | 22 | 21 | 17 | 13 |
| 25 | 29 | 10 | 9 | 26 | 12 |
| 36 | 5 | 33 | 4 | 2 | 31 |

*Number of Squares = 36; Row/Column total = 111; Square total = 666*

**Venus**

| | | | | | | |
|---|---|---|---|---|---|---|
| 22 | 47 | 16 | 41 | 10 | 35 | 4 |
| 5 | 23 | 48 | 17 | 42 | 11 | 29 |
| 30 | 6 | 24 | 49 | 18 | 36 | 12 |
| 13 | 31 | 7 | 25 | 43 | 19 | 37 |
| 38 | 14 | 32 | 1 | 26 | 44 | 20 |
| 21 | 39 | 8 | 33 | 2 | 27 | 45 |
| 46 | 15 | 40 | 9 | 34 | 3 | 28 |

*Number of Squares = 49; Row/Column total = 175; Square total = 1225*

**Mercury**

| | | | | | | | |
|---|---|---|---|---|---|---|---|
| 8 | 58 | 59 | 5 | 4 | 62 | 63 | 1 |
| 49 | 15 | 14 | 52 | 53 | 11 | 10 | 56 |
| 41 | 23 | 22 | 44 | 48 | 19 | 18 | 45 |
| 32 | 34 | 35 | 29 | 25 | 38 | 39 | 28 |
| 40 | 26 | 27 | 37 | 36 | 30 | 31 | 33 |
| 17 | 47 | 46 | 20 | 21 | 43 | 42 | 24 |
| 9 | 55 | 54 | 12 | 13 | 51 | 50 | 16 |
| 64 | 2 | 3 | 61 | 60 | 6 | 7 | 57 |

*Number of Squares = 64; Row/Column total = 260; Square total = 2080*

**Moon**

| | | | | | | | | |
|---|---|---|---|---|---|---|---|---|
| 37 | 78 | 29 | 70 | 21 | 62 | 13 | 54 | 5 |
| 6 | 38 | 79 | 30 | 71 | 22 | 63 | 14 | 46 |
| 47 | 7 | 39 | 80 | 31 | 72 | 23 | 55 | 15 |
| 16 | 48 | 8 | 40 | 81 | 32 | 64 | 24 | 56 |
| 57 | 17 | 49 | 9 | 41 | 73 | 33 | 65 | 25 |
| 26 | 58 | 18 | 50 | 1 | 42 | 74 | 34 | 66 |
| 67 | 27 | 59 | 10 | 51 | 2 | 43 | 75 | 35 |
| 36 | 68 | 19 | 60 | 11 | 52 | 3 | 44 | 76 |
| 77 | 28 | 69 | 20 | 61 | 12 | 53 | 4 | 45 |

*Number of Squares = 81; Row/Column total = 369; Square total = 3321*

David created the kameas for the trans-Saturnian planets in the 1980s using the same mathematical formula used to create the classical kameas. He did this so the same method of kamea sigilisation could be used for the outer planets. Uranus was attributed to the magickally appropriate 11x11 kamea. Neptune and Pluto were subsequently attributed to the 12x12 and 13x13 kameas respectively.

**Uranus**

| 56 | 117 | 46 | 107 | 36 | 97 | 26 | 87 | 16 | 77 | 6 |
|---|---|---|---|---|---|---|---|---|---|---|
| 7 | 57 | 118 | 47 | 108 | 37 | 98 | 27 | 88 | 17 | 67 |
| 68 | 8 | 58 | 119 | 48 | 109 | 38 | 99 | 28 | 78 | 18 |
| 19 | 69 | 9 | 59 | 120 | 49 | 110 | 39 | 89 | 29 | 79 |
| 80 | 20 | 70 | 10 | 60 | 121 | 50 | 100 | 40 | 90 | 30 |
| 31 | 81 | 21 | 71 | 11 | 61 | 111 | 51 | 101 | 41 | 91 |
| 92 | 32 | 82 | 22 | 72 | 1 | 62 | 112 | 52 | 102 | 42 |
| 43 | 93 | 33 | 83 | 12 | 73 | 2 | 63 | 113 | 53 | 103 |
| 104 | 44 | 94 | 23 | 84 | 13 | 74 | 3 | 64 | 114 | 54 |
| 55 | 105 | 34 | 95 | 24 | 85 | 14 | 75 | 4 | 65 | 115 |
| 116 | 45 | 106 | 35 | 96 | 25 | 86 | 15 | 76 | 5 | 66 |

*Number of Squares = 121; Row/Column total = 671; Square total = 7381*

**Neptune**

| 12 | 134 | 135 | 5 | 4 | 138 | 139 | 8 | 9 | 142 | 143 | 1 |
|---|---|---|---|---|---|---|---|---|---|---|---|
| 121 | 23 | 22 | 128 | 129 | 19 | 18 | 124 | 125 | 15 | 14 | 132 |
| 109 | 34 | 34 | 116 | 117 | 31 | 30 | 112 | 113 | 27 | 26 | 120 |
| 48 | 98 | 99 | 41 | 40 | 102 | 103 | 45 | 44 | 106 | 107 | 37 |
| 60 | 86 | 87 | 53 | 52 | 90 | 91 | 57 | 56 | 94 | 95 | 49 |
| 73 | 71 | 70 | 80 | 81 | 67 | 66 | 76 | 77 | 63 | 62 | 84 |
| 61 | 83 | 82 | 69 | 69 | 79 | 78 | 64 | 65 | 75 | 74 | 72 |
| 96 | 50 | 51 | 89 | 88 | 54 | 55 | 93 | 92 | 58 | 59 | 85 |
| 108 | 38 | 39 | 101 | 100 | 42 | 43 | 105 | 104 | 46 | 47 | 97 |
| 25 | 119 | 118 | 32 | 33 | 115 | 114 | 28 | 29 | 111 | 110 | 36 |
| 13 | 131 | 130 | 20 | 21 | 127 | 126 | 16 | 17 | 123 | 122 | 24 |
| 144 | 2 | 3 | 137 | 136 | 6 | 7 | 141 | 140 | 10 | 11 | 133 |

*Number of Squares = 144; Row/Column total = 870; Square total = 10440*

## Pluto

| 79 | 164 | 67 | 152 | 55 | 140 | 43 | 128 | 31 | 116 | 19 | 104 | 7 |
|---|---|---|---|---|---|---|---|---|---|---|---|---|
| 8 | 80 | 165 | 68 | 153 | 56 | 141 | 44 | 129 | 32 | 117 | 20 | 92 |
| 93 | 9 | 81 | 166 | 69 | 154 | 57 | 142 | 45 | 130 | 33 | 105 | 21 |
| 22 | 94 | 10 | 82 | 167 | 70 | 155 | 58 | 143 | 46 | 118 | 34 | 106 |
| 107 | 23 | 95 | 11 | 83 | 168 | 71 | 156 | 59 | 131 | 47 | 119 | 35 |
| 36 | 108 | 24 | 96 | 12 | 84 | 169 | 72 | 144 | 60 | 132 | 48 | 120 |
| 121 | 37 | 109 | 25 | 97 | 13 | 85 | 157 | 73 | 145 | 61 | 133 | 49 |
| 50 | 122 | 38 | 110 | 26 | 98 | 1 | 86 | 158 | 74 | 146 | 62 | 134 |
| 135 | 51 | 123 | 39 | 111 | 14 | 99 | 2 | 87 | 159 | 75 | 147 | 63 |
| 64 | 136 | 52 | 124 | 27 | 112 | 15 | 100 | 3 | 88 | 160 | 76 | 148 |
| 149 | 65 | 137 | 40 | 125 | 28 | 113 | 16 | 101 | 4 | 89 | 161 | 77 |
| 78 | 150 | 53 | 138 | 41 | 126 | 29 | 114 | 17 | 102 | 5 | 90 | 162 |
| 163 | 66 | 151 | 54 | 139 | 42 | 127 | 30 | 115 | 18 | 103 | 6 | 91 |

*Number of Squares = 169; Row/Column total = 1105; Square total = 14365*

APPENDIX 3

# Sigils for Planetary Intelligences & Spirits

In the context of the Planetary Intelligences and Spirits, it would probably be best to describe the sigils in respect of their roles. Using the sigil of the Planetary Spirit is creating a channel for the unfocused planetary energy to enter into your amulet or talisman and empower it. Adding the sigil of the Planetary Intelligence (or archangel) functions as a lens so that you are only getting completely focused planetary energy empowering your amulet or talisman.

When you look at these sigils, first recorded by Agrippa in his *Three Book of Occult Philosophy*, you will notice that he does not always abide by the rules he described! He sometimes reduces numbers when he does not need to, and where a name contains the letters IA together, which is common in names of spiritual creatures, the numerical values of the letters, I=10 and A=1, are often added to make 11, instead of using the squares for 10 and 1. In this instance a line is drawn to the square containing 11 and the two letters (IA) which make this numerical value are represented by a double loop to show their presence before the line is drawn to the next appropriate square.

## a. Kamea Sigils for the Seven Archangels

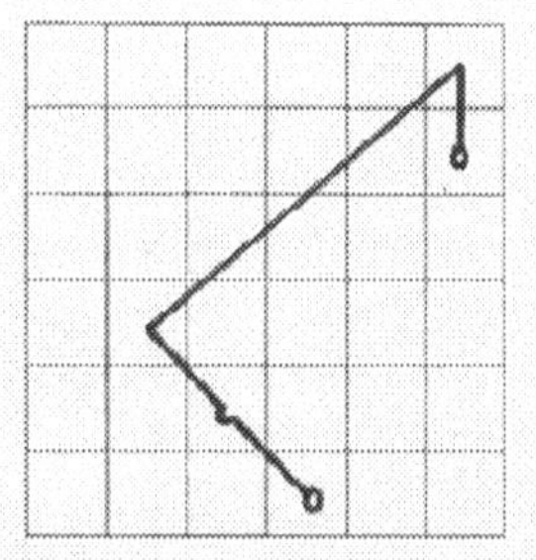

Michael - Archangel of the Sun

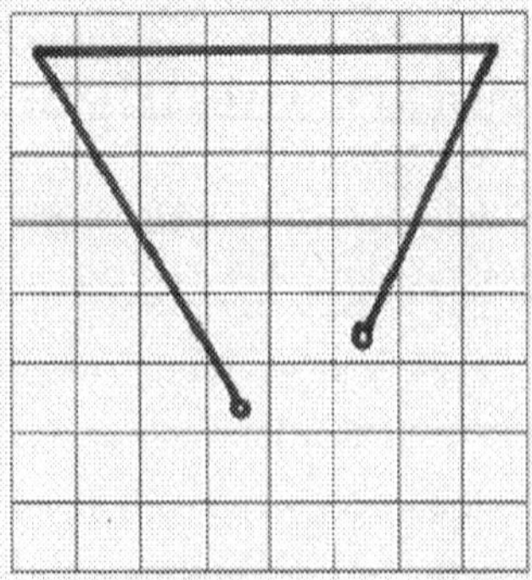

Raphael – Archangel of Mercury

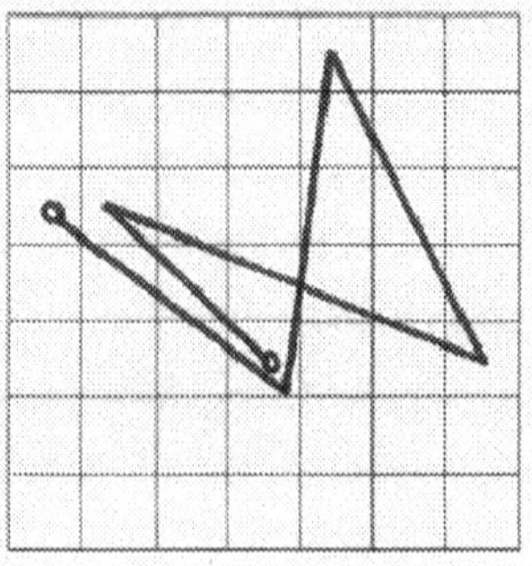

Uriel – Archangel of Venus

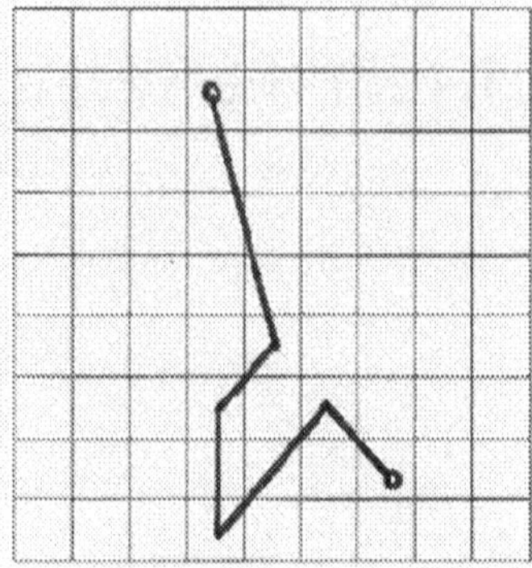

Gabriel – Archangel of the Moon

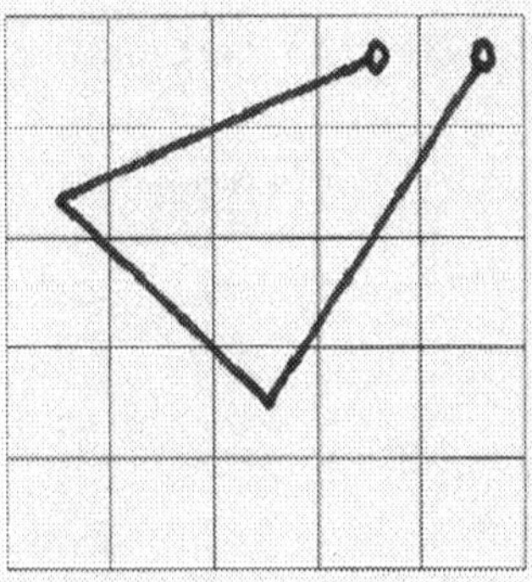

Khamael – Archangel of Mars

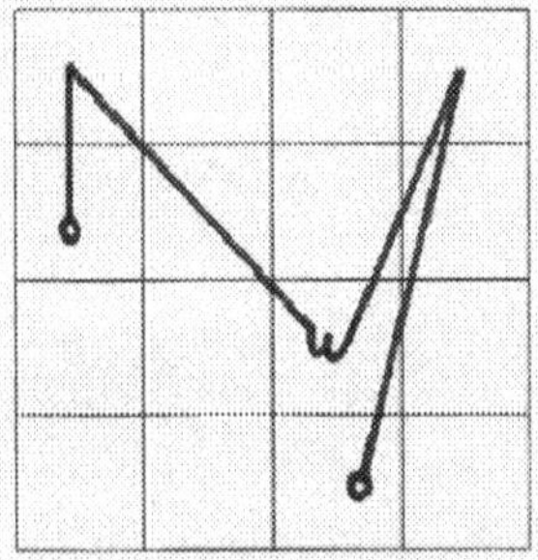

Tzadkiel – Archangel of Jupiter

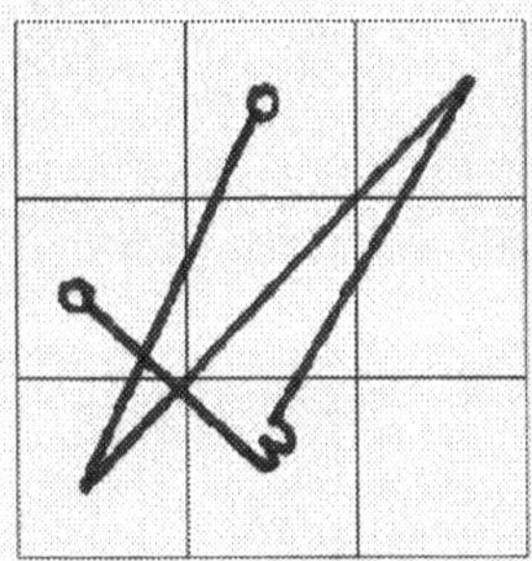

Tzaphkiel – Archangel of Saturn

# b. Kamea Sigils for the Planetary Intelligences

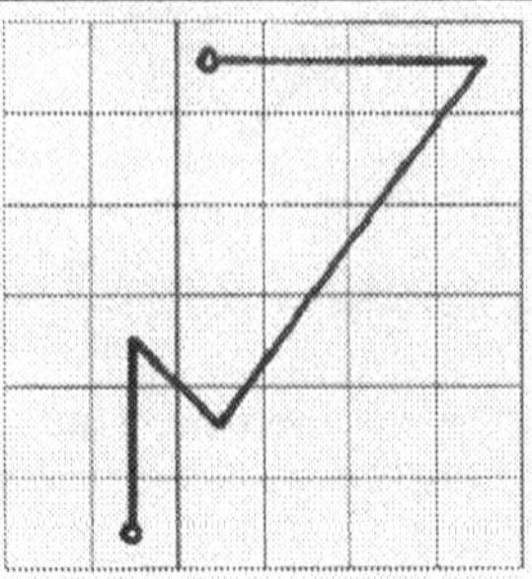

Nakhiel – Planetary Intelligence of the Sun

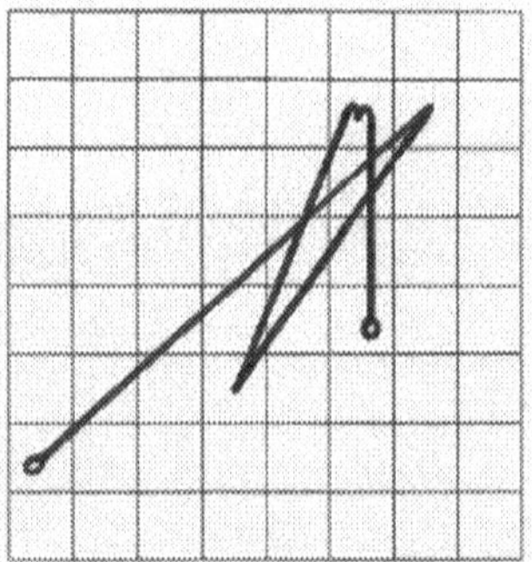

Tiriel – Planetary Intelligence of Mercury

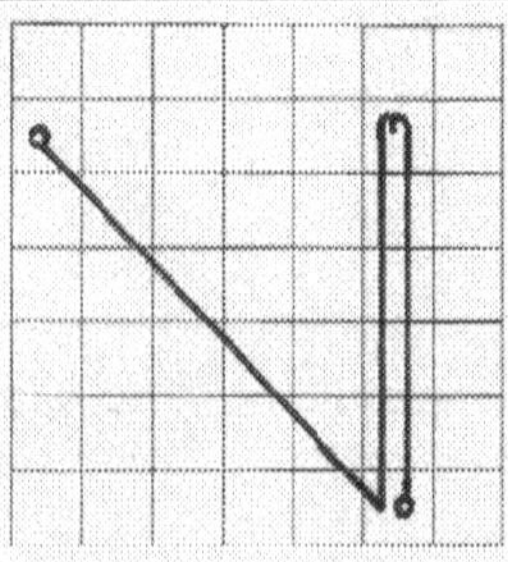

Hagiel – Planetary Intelligence of Venus

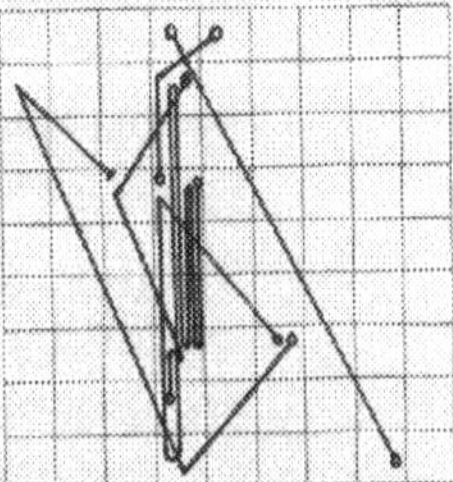

Malka – Planetary Intelligence of Intelligences of the Moon

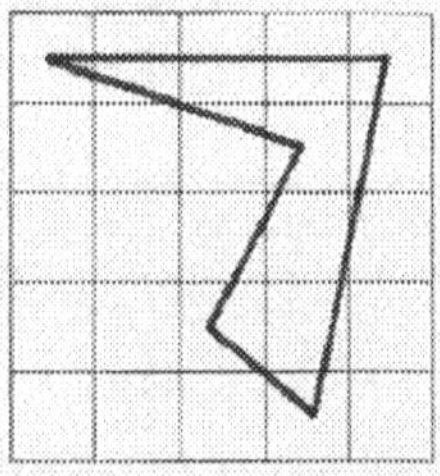

Graphiel – Planetary Intelligence of Mars

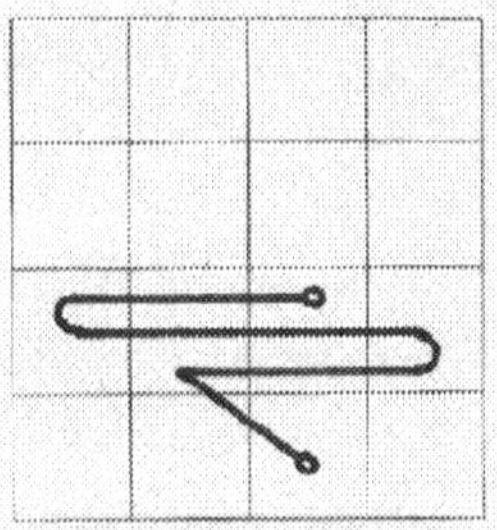

Jophiel – Planetary Intelligence of Jupiter

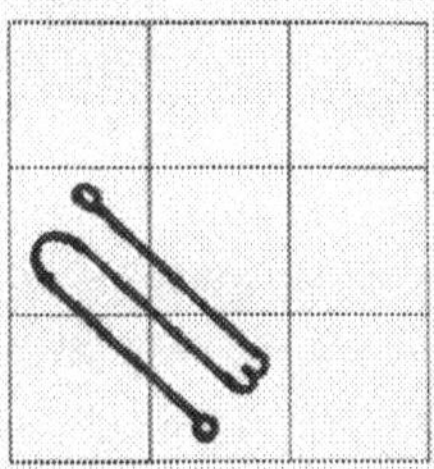

Agiel – Planetary Intelligence of Saturn

# c. Kamea Sigils of the Planetary Spirits

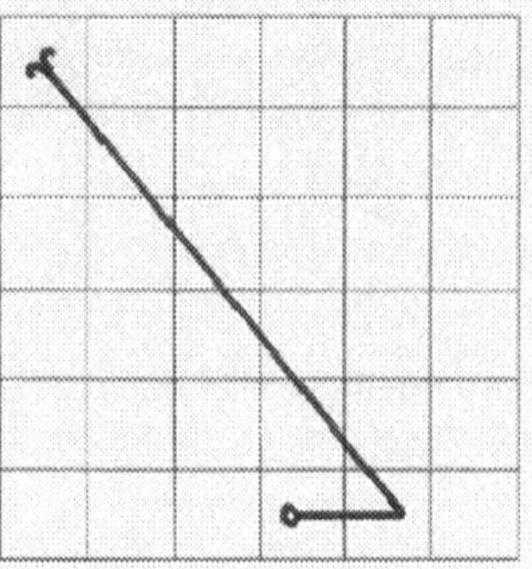

Sorath – Planetary Spirit of the Sun

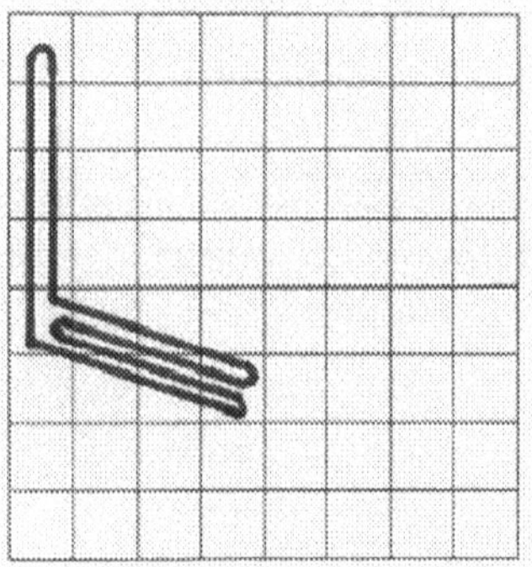

Taphthartharath – Planetary Spirit of Mercury

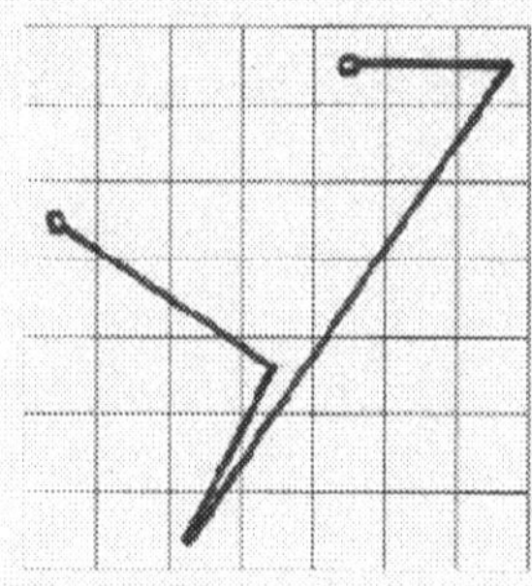

Kedemel – Planetary Spirit of Venus

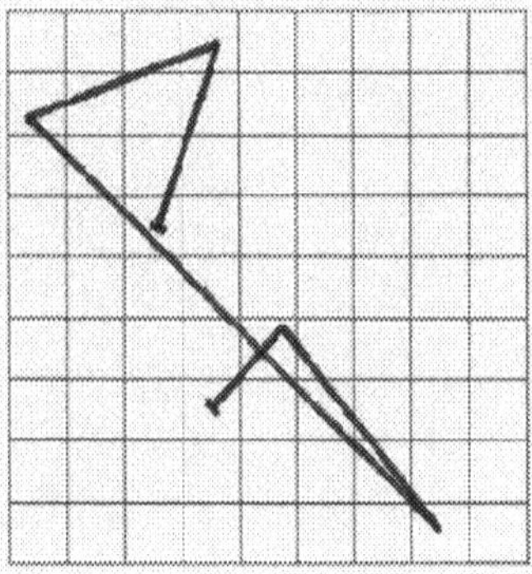

Chasmodai – Planetary Spirit of the Moon

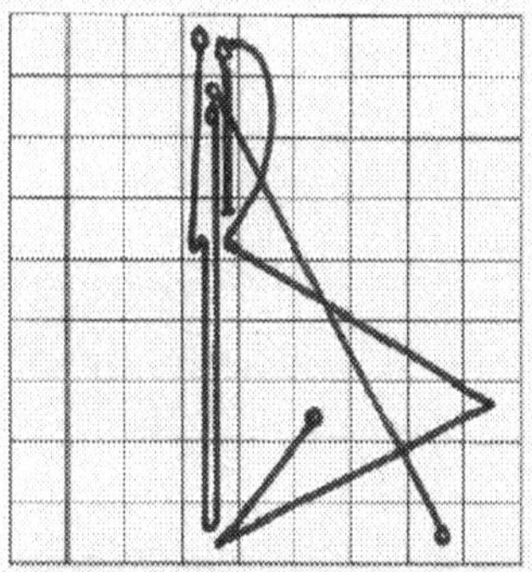

Schad – Planetary Spirit of Spirits of the Moon

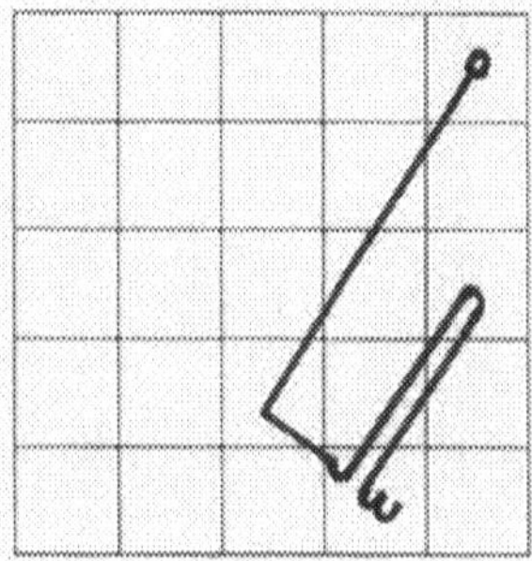

Bartzabel – Planetary Spirit of Mars

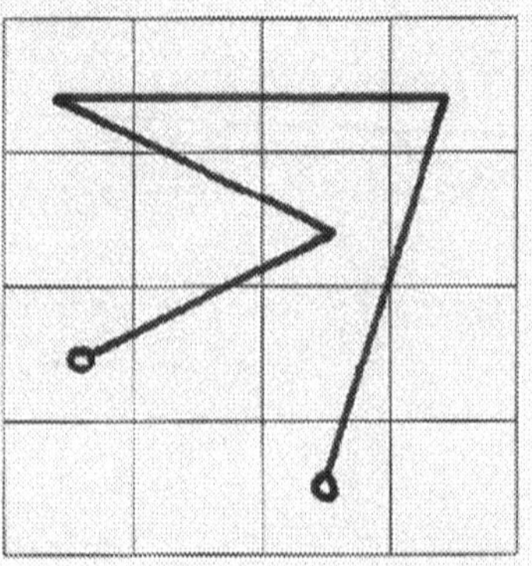

Hismael – Planetary Spirit of Jupiter

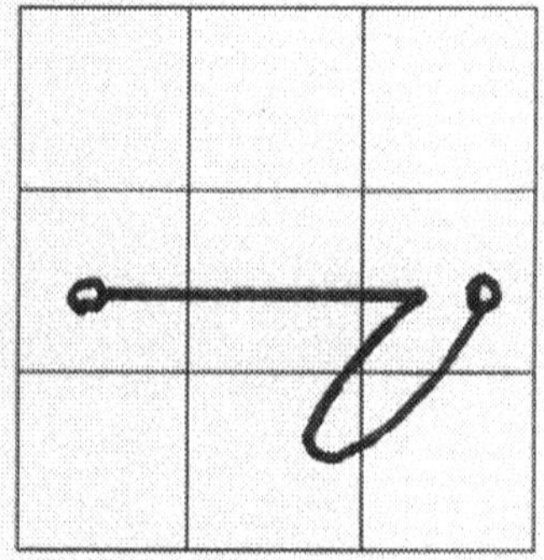

Zazel – Planetary Spirit of Saturn

APPENDIX 4

# Hebrew Names

Hebrew words associated with the planets are frequently used in talismans and other planetary magick. In consideration of this we have included the commonly used Hebrew words and their translations. These names include Qabalistic terms, such as the names of the planetary Sephiroth, their associated Divine Names and the names of the planets, and other commonly used titles. Additionally the names of the appropriate archangels, orders of angels, planetary intelligences and planetary spirits are also included.

| Hebrew | English |
|---|---|
| **The Sun** | |
| תפארת | Tiphereth |
| שמש | Shamash |
| סורת | Sorath |
| יהוה אלוה ודעת | Yahveh Eloah va-Daath |
| מלכים | Malakhim |
| נכיאל | Nakhiel |
| מיכאל | Michael |
| מלך | Melekh |
| אלוה | Eloah |

| Hebrew | English |
|---|---|
| | **Mercury** |
| תפתרתרת | Taphthartharath |
| אל ימ צבאות | Elohim Tzabaoth |
| רפאל | Raphael |
| טיריאל | Tiriel |
| בני אלהים | Bene Elohim |
| כוכו | Kokhav |
| הוד | Hod |
| | **Venus** |
| יהוה צבאות | Yahveh Tzabaoth |
| אוריאל | Uriel |
| קדמאל | Kedemel |
| נצח | Netzach |
| אלהים | Elohim |
| אנאל | Anael |
| נוגה | Nogah |
| הגיאל | Hagiel |
| | **The Moon** |
| מלכא בתרשישמ ועד ברוה שהרימ | Malka Be-Tarshishim ve-ad be-Ruah Sheharim |
| שד ברשהמעת השרתתנ | Shad Barshehmoth ha-Shartathan |
| חשמודאי | Chasmodai |
| שדי אל חי | Shaddai El Chai |
| שדי | Shaddai |
| כרובימ | Kerubim |
| גבריאל | Gabriel |
| לבנה | Levanah |
| יסוד | Yesod |

| Hebrew | English |
|---|---|
| **Mars** | |
| שרפים | Seraphim |
| גראפיאל | Graphiel |
| ברצבאל | Bartzabel |
| אלהים גבור | Elohim Gibor |
| גבורה | Geburah |
| מאדים | Madim |
| פחד | Pachad |
| כמאל | Khamael |
| אדני | Adonai |
| דין | Din |
| **Jupiter** | |
| חשמלים | Chasmalim |
| שחיאל | Sachiel |
| צדקיאל | Tzadkiel |
| צדק | Tzedeq |
| יופיל | Jophiel |
| הסמאל | Hismael |
| חסד | Chesed |
| גדולה | Gedulah |
| אל אב | El Ab |
| אל | El |
| יהוה | Yahveh |
| אבא | Aba |

| Hebrew | English |
| --- | --- |
| **Saturn** | |
| שבתאי | Shabathai |
| אראלימ | Aralim |
| צפכיאל | Tzaphkiel |
| יהוה אלהימ | Yahveh Elohim |
| בינה | Binah |
| אימא | Aima |
| אגיאל | Agiel |
| זאזל | Zazel |
| אמא | Ama |
| יה | Yah |

APPENDIX 5

# Planetary Fragrances

Writings from Mesopotamia mention seven planetary fragrances associated with the classical planets and their gods. These fragrances are Calamus, Cedar, Cypress, Galbanum, Labdanum, Myrtle and Storax. However as the references are fragmentary, the only specific associations we can be certain of amongst these plants are Cedar as being sacred to Marduk (and hence Jupiter) and Myrtle as being sacred to Shamash (and hence the Sun).

This theme of attributing specific scents to planetary gods was continued in ancient Greece. A reference in the *Greek Magickal Papyri* gives us a set of planetary attributions by listing specifically the seven Greek gods who were associated with the classical planets and their scents.

*"The proper incense of Kronos is storax, for it is heavy and fragrant; of Zeus, malabathron; of Ares, kostos; of Helios, frankincense; of Aphrodite, Indian nard; of Hermes, cassia; of Selene, myrrh."*[30]

| Planet | Incense Plant | Latin Name |
|---|---|---|
| Sun | Frankincense | Boswellia carterii |
| Mercury | Cassia | Cinnamomum cassia |
| Venus | Spikenard | Nardostachys jatamansi |
| Moon | Myrrh | Commiphora myrrha |
| Mars | Kostos | Sassurea lappa |
| Jupiter | Malabathron (Indian Bay Leaf) | Cinnamomum tamala |
| Saturn | Storax | Liquidambar styraciflua L. |

30 PGM XIII.17-20.

By the time of the Grimoires different sets of fragrances were being attributed, based on availability and also a very different cultural situation, where the planets were no longer being worshipped as different gods, but as part of the Christian creation. Thus if we compare scents given in Agrippa's *Three Books of Occult Philosophy* (published 1531-3) and the *Heptameron* (published 1485) we see the following attributions:

| Planet | Heptameron | Agrippa |
|---|---|---|
| Sun | Red Sandalwood[31] | Mastic |
| Mercury | Mastic | Cinnamon |
| Venus | Pepperwort | Saffron |
| Moon | Aloes | Myrtle |
| Mars | Pepper | Lignum Aloes |
| Jupiter | Saffron | Nutmeg |
| Saturn | Sulphur | Pepperwort |

The incenses given by Agrippa for working with the planets include animal blood and brains, and are not of a type that any modern practitioner would be comfortable with making, smelling or using!

For Evocation, censers of incense were often placed at the points of the triangle to provide a reasonable quantity of incense smoke over the triangle to act as a medium, giving the demon a physical basis to manifest in. This use of incense was entirely in keeping with the belief that demons were formed from the element of Air, giving them a *"thicker"* form of Air to create an appearance in.

---

31 The translation reads "Red Wheat", which we have taken as being an error, and this as the most likely original attribution.

APPENDIX 6

# The Planets and Minerals

*"Make the Sun gold, the Moon silver, Kronos of obsidian, Ares of yellow-green onyx, Aphrodite of lapis lazuli streaked with gold, Hermes of turquoise, make Zeus of a dark blue stone, but underneath of crystal."* [32]

As this quote from the *Greek Magical Papyri* shows, there is along history of association between minerals and the planets. Agrippa, in his classic *Three Books of Occult Philosophy* lists minerals associated with each of the planets. This list is given below, though we may note that many of the minerals are repeated for at least two (or even three) of the planets, which does limit the value of his list, despite its regular duplication and common use in the subsequent five hundred years.

| Planet | Agrippa |
|---|---|
| Sun | Cats Eye (Oculus Solis), Chrysoprase, Garnet (Carbuncle), Gold, Heliotrope, Peridot (Chrysolite), Rainbow Quartz, Ruby, Topaz, Zircon (Hyacinth) |
| Mercury | Agate (Achates), Emerald, Marcasite, Mercury (Quicksilver), Red Marble, Tin, Topaz |
| Venus | Beryl, Brass, Carnelian (Corneola), Coral, Emerald, Green Jasper, Lapis Lazuli, Peridot (Chrysolite), Sapphire, Silver |
| Moon | Beryl, Marcasite, Moonstone (Selenites), Pearl, Quartz (Crystal), Silver |
| Mars | Amethyst, Bloodstone, Brass, Diamond, Iron, Jasper, Magnetite (Lodestone) |
| Jupiter | Beryl, Emerald, Gold, Green Jasper, Sapphire, Silver, Tin, Zircon (Hyacinth) |
| Saturn | Brown Jasper, Chalcedony, Gold, Lead, Magnetite (Lodestone), Onyx, Pyrites (Golden Marcasite), Sapphire |

32 PGM CX.4-11.

For convenience we have included a list of attributions which is more rationalised than Agrippa, drawing on a range of classical sources for their associations. We would recommend this list as a more appropriate source for your choice of planetary minerals for magickal work.

| Planet | Minerals |
|---|---|
| Sun | Amber, Cats Eye, Chrysoprase, Diamond, Gold, Heliotrope, Peridot, Sunstone, Tigers Eye, Topaz, Zircon |
| Mercury | Agate, Aventurine, Citrine Quartz, Labradorite, Mercury, Opal |
| Venus | Amazonite, Copper, Emerald, Jadeite, Lapis Lazuli, Malachite, Nephrite, Peridot, Rose Quartz, Zoisite |
| Moon | Aquamarine, Beryl, Chalcedony, Gypsum, Ivory, Moonstone, Pearl, Quartz, Selenite, Silver |
| Mars | Bloodstone, Brass, Carnelian, Garnet, Hematite, Iron, Magnetite, Pyrites, Ruby, Spinel |
| Jupiter | Amethyst, Ammonite, Azurite, Sapphire, Sodalite, Tin, Turquoise |
| Saturn | Coral, Jet, Lead, Obsidian, Onyx, Serpentine, Smoky Quartz |

APPENDIX 7

# The Planets and Plants

Plants have long been associated with the planets. Through their scents, used to please the gods; their healing uses and their shapes an colours, plants have become a major symbol of the axiom of *"as above, so below"*, reflecting in nature physical qualities associated with the wandering stars in the heavens.

| Planet | Vegetable |
|---|---|
| The Sun | Acacia, Angelica, Ash (Tree), Balsam, Bay, Butter-bur, Calamus, Chamomile, Celandine, Centaury, Cinnamon, Eyebright, Frankincense, Galangal, Gentian, Ginger, Gorse, Heliotrope, Hyacinth, Juniper, Marigold, Mistletoe, Oak, Orange, Orris, Palm, Peony, Pine, Saffron, St Johns Wort, Storax, Sunflower, Vine, Walnut |
| Mercury | Caraway, Dill, Eucalyptus, Herb Mercury, Lavender, Lemon, Lime, Liquorice, Mace, Marjoram, Mastic, Moly, Sandalwood, Storax, Tragacanth |
| Venus | Adam & Eve Root, Balm, Benzoin, Bergamot, Clover, Daffodil, Elder, Geranium, Lady's Mantle, Lilac, Myrtle, Pennyroyal, Peppermint, Primrose, Rose, Saunderswood, Sycamore, Venus Fly Trap, Violet |
| Moon | Adders Tongue, Alder, Aniseed, Artemisia, Camphor, Hazel, Honeysuckle, Jasmine, Jojoba, Lignum Aloes, Mangrove, Moonwort, Ranunculus, Thyme, Turmeric, Willow, Witchazel, Ylang Ylang |
| Mars | Basil, Bay, Black Pepper, Buttercup, Capsicum, Chilli, Dragons Blood, Ginger, Hickory, Mustard, Nettle, Opoponax, Pepper, Rue, Thistle, Tobacco |
| Jupiter | Agrimony, Alfalfa, Alkanet, Arnica, Bayberry, Betony, Borage, Cedar, Chervil, Cinquefoil, Copal, Dock, Fir, Fumitory, Hyssop, Maple, Melissa, Poplar, Saffron, Sage, Shamrock, St John's Wort, Vervain |
| Saturn | Aconite, Asafoetida, Belladonna, Civet, Cypress, Datura, Hellebore, Hemlock, Henbane, Myrrh, Yew |

APPENDIX 8

# The Planets & Mankind

The ancients attributed rulership of different parts of the body to the planets. This association of the planets to the body was known as melothesic (zodiacal) man. By working with the appropriate planets, healing work was performed on the body. These attributions developed into the subsequent astrological rulership of parts of the body by the twelve astrological signs.

Likewise the planets were also attributed to the periods of human life, known as the Seven Ages of Man. This is referred to by Shakespeare in his famous quote in *As You Like It* (II.viii), which begins with the line *"All the world's a stage, and all the men and women merely players"*. He gives the seven ages as being the infant, the school-boy, the lover, the soldier, the justice, old age and the lead-up to death, which clearly correspond to the classic planetary associations.

| Planet | Melothesic Man | Planetary Age | Virtue |
|---|---|---|---|
| Sun | Sense of Sight, Right-hand Side, Brain, Heart, Sinews | Fourth Age of Man which is 23-41 years | Virility |
| Mercury | Speech & Thought, Bile, Buttocks, Tongue | Second Age of Man which is 5-14 years | Education |
| Venus | Sense of Smell, Liver, Flesh | Third Age of Man which is 15-22 years | Emotion |
| Moon | Sense of Taste, Left-hand Side, Belly, Stomach, Womb | First Age of Man which is birth to 4 years old. | Growth |
| Mars | Genitals, Kidneys, Left Ear, Veins | Fifth Age of Man which is 42-56 years | Ambition |
| Jupiter | Sense of Touch, Arteries, Lungs, semen | Sixth Age of Man which is 57-68 years | Reflection |
| Saturn | Bladder, Bones, Phlegm, Right Ear, Spleen | Seventh Age of Man, which is 69 years to end of life | Resignation |

APPENDIX 9

# The Planets and Animals

The characteristics and behaviour of animals has over the centuries resulted in their being used as symbols of deities and planetary energies. This was particularly evident in ancient Egypt, where many of the deities had animal or composite human-animal forms. From these early associations planetary symbolism for animals became a common form of representation, even of shorthand, such as an eagle representing Zeus or Jupiter rather than showing the god himself. The Greek and Roman deities continued this theme, with deities assuming sacred animal forms on occasions.

| Planet | Animal |
|---|---|
| Sun | Bee, Falcon, Hawk, Leopard, Lion, Pelican, Phoenix, Puma, Sparrowhawk, Swan, Tiger |
| Mercury | Ape, Baboon, Bat, Coyote, Dog, Hermaphrodite, Hummingbird, Kingfisher, Jackal, Jay, Magpie, Parrot, Salmon, Swallow, Twin Serpents |
| Venus | Birds, Dove, Lynx, Nightingale, Partridge, Peacock, Pigeon, Sow, Sparrow |
| Moon | Badger, Cat, Crab, Deer, Dog, Elephant, Frog, Hare, Heron, Hyena, Lizards, Otter, Owl, Rat, Snail, Stork, Toad, Tortoise, Unicorn |
| Mars | Basilisk, Bear, Boar, Cock, Hippogrif, Horse, Ram, Wolf, Woodpecker |
| Jupiter | Bull, Centaur, Cuckoo, Eagle, Goose, Gryphon, Praying Mantis, Ram, Raven, Stag, Sturgeon, Wren |
| Saturn | Ass, Cow, Crocodile, Crow, Donkey, Goat, Hippopotamus, Mole, Raven |

APPENDIX 10

# Planetary Sigils

The alchemical and hermetic writings of the Middle Ages and Renaissance contained a whole host of sigils for the classical planets. The sigils that have become accepted as the standard were reproduced in the Italian publication of Hyginus' *"Poeticon Astronomicon"* in 1482 CE.

The planetary sigils are all made from combinations of three constituent symbols, the circle, the crescent and the equal-armed cross. Which symbols form the planetary sigil, and the positioning of the component symbols tells you a great deal about the nature of the energy of the planet.

## Sun

The Solar sigil is a circle with a dot in the centre. The circle represents the life-giving energies of the infinite, the cycle of life, death and rebirth.

The dot in the centre emphasises the primal nature of these energies, reflected in the level of solar worship throughout history and the vital nature of the sun for life on earth. The absence of anything connected to the circle indicates the way the solar energy emanates universally, as is sometimes shown by rays coming off the circle in all directions.

## Mercury

The sigil of Mercury shows a circle atop an equal-armed cross, with a crescent horns up intersecting the top of the circle. Here the life essence of the circle is conjoined with the crescent of time, dominating the cross of matter.

The union of time and life emphasises the quicksilver nature of Mercury, speeding over the elemental cross. As the crescent only slightly touches the circle, it can be seen that Mercury's influence is one of subtlety rather than direct action.

## Venus

The sigil of Venus depicts a circle atop an equal-armed cross. The life-giving energies of the circle dominate the cross of matter. This form shows the power of Venus as the force of generation and attraction, with the essence of life dominating the physical world.

## Moon

The sigil of the Moon is a crescent usually facing to the left, or occasionally to the right. The cyclic nature of the Moon is entirely indicated by its symbol of the crescent, which changes form through every part of the lunar cycle.

## Mars

The sigil of Mars shows a circle with an arrow connected to it at the NE point of the circle. It emphasises the energy and vitality of Mars, with the life-giving circle expressing its energy through action, indicated by the arrow being at a diagonal and to the upper right (corresponding to the right arm and hand, the dominant active force in most people). Modern writers have equated this symbol to a shield and lance, emphasising the warrior qualities of Mars.

## Jupiter

The sigil of Jupiter is an equal-armed cross with a left-facing crescent joined to the left-hand arm of the cross by its bottom tip. Although the sigil is made of the same components as the Saturn sigil, the emphasis here is on expansion rather than contraction, with the crescent facing outwards, expressing the balance of form outwards in time producing change, rather than limiting it inwards to a static state.

## Saturn

The sigil of Saturn is formed of an equal-armed cross with a left-facing crescent attached to the bottom of the cross by its upper tip. This symbolically expresses the qualities of Saturn, with the equal-armed cross of matter and form dominating the crescent which represents time in the context of the lunar cycle of ebb and flow.

The Saturn sigil is thus one of solidity and its restriction.

**APPENDIX 11**

# Planetary Contemplations

## Sun

Close your eyes and visualise the Sun symbol in gold on a purple background. As you visualise the golden circle with its central golden dot, contemplate the solar qualities of egotism, friendship, joy, success, wealth and will. How strong are each of these forces in your life?

Which of them are you actively trying to cultivate or transform? What other qualities or events do they bring to mind as you contemplate their influences?

## Mercury

Close your eyes and visualise the Mercury symbol in orange on a blue background. As you visualise the orange circle on top of the orange equal-armed cross, surmounted by the orange crescent with its horns up, contemplate the Mercurial qualities of communication, deception, flexibility, magick, memory and speed.

How strong are each of these forces in your life? Which of them are you actively trying to cultivate or transform? What other qualities or events do they bring to mind as you contemplate their influences?

## Venus

Close your eyes and visualise the Venus symbol in green on a red background. As you visualise the emerald green circle on top of the emerald green equal-armed cross, contemplate the Venusian qualities of beauty, culture, fertility, love, sexuality and sociability.

How strong are each of these forces in your life? Which of them are you actively trying to cultivate or transform? What other qualities or events do they bring to mind as you contemplate their influences?

## Moon

Close your eyes and visualise the Moon symbol in silver on a yellow background. As you visualise the silver crescent facing to the left, contemplate the Lunar qualities of clairvoyance, dreams, glamour, spirituality, transformation, and your unconscious.

How strong are each of these forces in your life? Which of them are you actively trying to cultivate or transform? What other qualities or events do they bring to mind as you contemplate their influences?

## Mars

Close your eyes and visualise the Mars symbol in red on a green background. As you visualise the scarlet red circle with the scarlet red arrow coming out of the upper right (NE) of the circle, contemplate the Martial qualities of anger, courage, passion, strength, vengeance and vigour.

How strong are each of these forces in your life? Which of them are you actively trying to cultivate or transform? What other qualities or events do they bring to mind as you contemplate their influences?

## Jupiter

Close your eyes and visualise the Jupiter symbol in blue on an orange background. As you visualise the sapphire blue equal-armed cross with the sapphire blue crescent facing left joined to the leftmost tip of the horizontal bar of the cross, contemplate the Jupiterian qualities of authority, ethics, fortune, humour, responsibility and truth.

How strong are each of these forces in your life? Which of them are you actively trying to cultivate or transform? What other qualities or events do they bring to mind as you contemplate their influences?

## Saturn

Close your eyes and visualise the Saturn symbol in black on a white background. As you visualise the black equal-armed cross with the black left-facing crescent attached to the bottom of the cross, contemplate the Saturnian qualities of austerity, duty, equilibrium, limitation, patience and self-discipline.

How strong are each of these forces in your life? Which of them are you actively trying to cultivate or transform? What other qualities or events do they bring to mind as you contemplate their influences?

APPENDIX 12

# Invocation of Planetary Intelligences

This conjuration is a template of the conjurations of the Planetary Intelligences found in *Sloane MSS 3821.* The conjurations are all identical except for the name of the Planetary Intelligence, the Divine Names it responds to and the associated planet. In the sections on the Spiritual Creatures of the Planets, there are Divine Names given which the Intelligence responds to, these are the ones which should be incorporated into this conjuration if you decide to use it. So, e.g. for Saturn you would be calling the Planetary Intelligence Agiel, and the Divine Names he responds to are Ab, Hod, Yah, Hod, Yahveh

*"O You benevolent Intelligence, of Celestial light, Dignified, & by Nature Angelical, who art Known or called, by the name, [Intelligence Name]: & said to be of the Nature & office, of the planet or Star Called [Planet], When by Celestial position it shall, be both Essentially & Accidentally Well Dignified, and fortified with all Others your Substitutes the president Intelligences, or Dignified powers of Light properly Residing in Or Otherwise Appertaining to your Mansion Orders or Hierarchy from the Superior to the Inferior and Serving the most High God in your Respective Orders & office as Mediums of Divine Grace and Mercy, & as in Charge Command & Appointed we the Servants also of the Highest Reverently here present in his holy fear Do Earnestly, beseech humbly Request Strongly Invocate Call forth & powerfully move you to Visible Appearance in by & through these Excellent Ineffable great Signal Sacred & Divine Names of your God [Divine Names]: Even the Omnipotent Immortal Immense Incomprehensible & most high god and Lord of hosts Jehovah, before whom the whole Choir of heaven Continually Singeth, O Mappa:laman Hallelujah And by the Seal of your Creation being the Mark or Character of holiness unto you & by the great Mystery Virtue force power Efficacy and Influence, of all we Do Strongly Invocate Confidently Call forth & powerfully Move you O you Benevolent Intelligence or Angelical Medium of Light Celestially Dignified who by*

*name are Called [Name] with all Others the president & Servient Angels or Mediums of Light Celestially Dignified by Degree & office in general & particular Every & Each one for & by it Self respectively appertaining to your Hierarchy mansion or place of residence to Visible Appearance; move therefore O ye Benevolent Intelligence, [Name], with all Others of your Orders office Hierarchy Or Mansion Jointly & Severally as aforesaid gird up & gather your Self or Selves Accordingly together & some one or more of you, as it shall please God of his Special grace & permission is given to you and also Accordingly Descend from your Mansion or place of Residence or wheresoever Else you may be Otherwise officiating or Chancely Absent therefrom and Immediately forthwith Appear Visibly, here before us in this Crystal Stone or Glass Receptacle Standing here before us & in & through the same to transmit your true and real presence In Splendid Appearance plainly unto the Light of our Eyes Utter your Voices unto our Ears that we may Not only Visibly see you but Audibly hear you Speak unto us and that we may Converse with you or otherwise forthwith Appear out of them Visible Upon this Table or Hereby upon the floor and Show plainly & visibly unto us A Sufficient Sign or test of your Coming and Appearance therefore we Do Entreat you and Undeniably Request you Charge Constrain Command and powerfully Move you O you Royal and Amicable Angel or Blessed Intelligence [Name] who art lately Ascribed to the planet [planet] and by the great Names of god governing that planet: [Divine Names]: God again and again powerfully without any delay Lingering or tarrying strictly charge that you descend Not one Minute Longer to Serve us and really fulfil all that is appropriated and belonging to your Charge Under the planet: [planet]: [Name]: Name]: Name]: gird up Move Come forth and faithfully Answer to all that belongs to your Hierarchy office or order I being Armed with power from above Name]: behold the Exorcism the Stamp of the very Idea the Microcosm: by: Agla: El: On; Tetragrammaton: by: Ogim Osj who Sitteth Upon the throne by all that hath been Now is and Ever Shall be by the paleigicks and prophets by the Great lamen Schemhamphorash by heaven Earth and hell [Name] thou blessed Intelligence of [planet] by All Aforesaid: Move: Move: Move: Come forth and Visibly Show thy self at this Very Minute as you will answer the Contrary being high Misdemeanour at your peril before him who Shall Come to Judge the quick and the Dead and the world by fire fiat fiat fiat for why we are Servants of the same your god, and true worshippers of the Highest, wherefore be friendly unto us and Do for us as for the Servants of the Highest whereunto In his Name we Do again Earnestly Request elegantly and undeniably Move you both in power and presence O you Royal Spirit [Name] whose friendship unto us herein and works Shall be a Song of honour and the praise of your god in your Creation. Amen."*

APPENDIX 13

# The Heptagram

The heptagram (sometimes called the *Septagram*) is the seven-pointed star which has been used by a number of magickal traditions. It has two forms, which are formally known as the 7/2 and 7/3 heptagram, the numbers 2 and 3 referring to the number of points you go around the star to draw the next line of the heptagram with the single continuous stroke that forms its shape. Both the 7/2 and 7/3 heptagram have been used by order such as the Golden Dawn as planetary emblems, with the seven classical planets and days of the week being attributed to the seven points of the star.

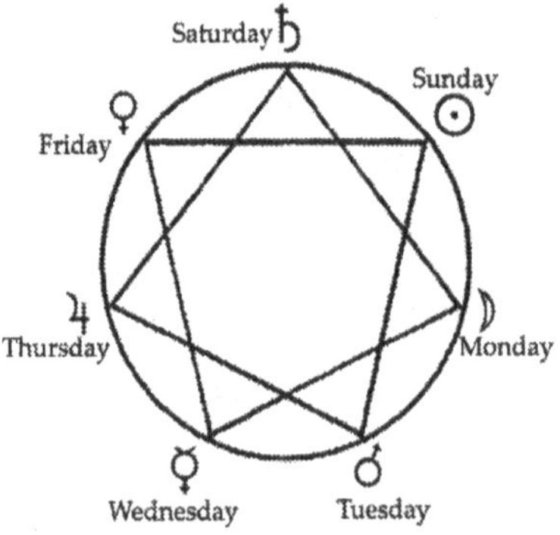


7/2 Heptagram showing Days of the Week

7/3 Heptagram

The 7/2 heptagram was popular in the grimoires, where it is seen in the famous Sigillum Dei Aemeth (*"Sigil of God's Truth"*) in the thirteenth century grimoire *Liber Juratus.* This image was adopted by Dr John Dee in the sixteenth century and used as a central part of his Enochian system of magick.

The 7/2 heptagram was also subsequently used by Aleister Crowley, who associated it with Babalon, the Scarlet Woman, and used it in the emblem of his magickal order the A.A. (*Astreum Argenteum* or Silver Star). The 7/3 heptagram was referred to by the Hermetic Order of the Golden Dawn as the *"Star of Venus"* (due to its seven points, seven being the Venusian number).

The table below indicates the associated planetary colours for the heptagrams associated with the respective planets, as well as the Greek vowel, sound and position on the heptagram.

| Vowel | Sound | Planet | Colour | Position |
|---|---|---|---|---|
| Alpha | A | Moon | Silver | Middle Right |
| Epsilon | E | Mercury | Orange | Bottom Left |
| Eta | Ē (EE) | Venus | Green | Upper Left |
| Iota | I | Sun | Gold | Upper Right |
| Omicron | O | Mars | Red | Bottom Right |
| Upsilon | U | Jupiter | Blue | Middle Left |
| Omega | Ō (OO) | Saturn | Black | Top |

The easy way to remember the positions of the planets on the points of the heptagram is by the days of the week, moving clockwise round from the top. The top point is Saturn (Saturday), upper right is Sun (Sunday), middle right is Moon (Monday), lower right is Mars (Tuesday), lower left is Mercury (Wednesday), middle left is Jupiter (Thursday), upper left is Venus (Friday)

APPENDIX 14

# Terms & Definitions

Terms such as invocation and evocation have gained different meanings over centuries of use, which can be confusing or even misleading if the context of their use is not clearly defined. For the purpose of this book we are giving our definitions of these terms and how they are applied to the planetary work within it.

## Hymns

A hymn is a spiritual song or lyrical religious poem. By its definition a hymn is a series of words, usually in adoration or praise of a deity. What we call a hymn is often referred to as invocation in modern pagan traditions, though by our definition this is not the case. A hymn does not include music, and when music is added to a hymn, it is the hymn tune.

Examples of hymns of this kind are the Egyptian *Great Hymn to the Aten* composed by the Pharaoh Akhenaten, and the *Homeric Hymns* to the Greek Gods. The hymns to the Planetary Gods within this book are based upon the Homeric Hymns in their style and content, rewritten in modern language.

## Conjuration

We use the term Conjuration to refer to the calling of a spiritual creature, as part of the process of Invocation or Evocation. Although some old texts refer to the long prose calls as invocations, to avoid confusion we are using the term Conjuration to refer to this part of the process.

## Invocation

We are defining Invocation as the process of calling of a deity or spiritual creature into something or someone. This then includes the use of crystal stones, glass receptacles, bowls of liquid and magick mirrors, statues as fetishes and techniques such as the Wiccan ceremony of *"Drawing Down the Moon"*, where a specific deity is called into a person who is awaiting this contact. The practical work with Olympic Spirits found later in the book is invocatory in its nature, being the calling of the Olympic Spirit to appear within a crystal.

## Evocation

Evocation is the process of calling forth of a spiritual creature to tangible presence. When evocation is to visible appearance it is in a medium provided to give form to the creature, usually incense. It does not apply to the appearance of an image of the creature in a receptacle such as a crystal or mirror, which we have defined as invocation.

A noteworthy difference between hymning and both invocation and evocation is that the former requires no appearance of the spiritual creature , whereas the latter two seek either an image of the creature in the case of invocation or a presence of the creature in the case of evocation.

# Bibliography


Agrippa, Cornelius, *Three Books of Occult Philosophy*, 2005, Llewellyn, Minnesota

-----------, *The Fourth Book of Occult Philosophy*, 1979, Askin Press, London

Barrett, Francis, *The Magus*, ND, IGOS, California

Barry, Kieren, *The Greek Qabalah*, 1999, Samuel Weiser Inc., Maine

Betz, Hans Dieter (ed), *The Greek Magical Papyri in Translation*, 1992, University of Chicago Press, Chicago

Bruno, Giordano, *De Imaginum Compositione*, 1591, www.esotericarchives.com

Butler, E.M., *Ritual Magic*, 1949, Cambridge University Press, Cambridge

Dariot, Claudius, *A Brief and most Easy Astrological Judgment of the Stars*, 1997 reprint, Spica Publications, Brisbane

Dionysus the Areopagite, *The Celestial Hierarchy*, 2004, Kessinger Publishing

Fanger, Claire (ed), *Conjuring Spirits: Texts and Traditions of Medieval Ritual Magic*, 1998, Sutton Publishing, Stroud

Faraone, Christopher A., & Obbink, Dirk (eds), *Magika Hiera: Ancient Greek Magic & Religion*, 1991, Oxford University Press, Oxford

Fischer-Rizzi, Susanne, *The Complete Incense Book*, 1998, Sterling Publishing Co, New York

Gettings, Fred, *Dictionary of Occult, Hermetic and Alchemical Sigils*, 1981, Routledge & Kegan Paul, London

------------, *The Arkana Dictionary of Astrology*, 1990, Arkana, London

Kaplan, Aryeh, *The Sepher Yetzirah*. 1997, Red Wheel/Weiser, Maine

Kerenyi, C., *The Gods of the Greeks*, 1951, Thames & Hudson, London

King, Francis & Skinner, Stephen, *Techniques of High Magic*, 1981, Sphere, London

Lisiewski, Joseph C., *Ceremonial Magic & The Power of Evocation*, 2004, New Falcon, Arizona

Mathers, S.L. MacGregor, *The Key of Solomon the King*, 2000, Samuel Weiser Inc, Maine

McLean, Adam (ed), *The Magical Calendar*, 1994, Phanes Press, Michigan

----------- (ed), *A Treatise on Angel Magic*, 1982, Hermetic Research Trust, Warwickshire

Meyer, Marvin W. & Smith, Richard, *Ancient Christian Magic, Coptic Texts of Ritual Power*, 1994, Princeton University Press, Princeton

Moore, Thomas, *The Planets Within: Marsilio Ficino's Astrological Psychology*, 1982, Associated University Presses Ltd, London

Neugebauer, O., *The Exact Sciences in Antiquity*, 1967, Dover, New York

Oken, Alan, *As Above, So Below*, 1973, Bantam Books Inc, New York

Rankine, David, *Becoming Magick*, 2004, Mandrake, Oxford

-----------, *Climbing the Tree of Life*, 2005, Avalonia, London

Regardie, Israel, *The Golden Dawn*, 1997, Llewellyn, Minnesota

Savedow, Steve (trans), *Sepher Rezial Hemelach: The Book of the Angel Rezial*, 2000, Samuel Weiser Inc, Maine

Shah, Idries, *The Secret Lore of Magic*, 1963, Frederick Muller Ltd, London

Skinner, Stephen, *The Complete Magician's Tables*, 2006, Golden Hoard Press, London

Skinner, Stephen & Rankine, David, *The Keys to the Gateway of Magic*, 2005, Golden Hoard Press, London

Taylor, Thomas (trans), *The Hymns of Orpheus*, 1792, London

-----------, (trans), *Iamblichus: On the Mysteries of the Egyptians, Chaldeans, and Assyrians*, 1968 (originally 1821), Stuart & Watkins, London

Vinci, Leo, *Summa Angelica*, 2003, Writersworld, Woodstock

Walker, D.P., *Spiritual & Demonic Magic from Ficino to Campanella*, 2000, Sutton Publishing Ltd, Stroud

## Source Manuscripts

Additional MSS 36674, 16th century, British Library, London

Cambridge MS Dd.xi.45, 1441-5, Cambridge Library, Cambridge

Harley MSS 6482, 1712, British Library, London

Lansdowne MSS 1202 & 3, 17th century, British Library, London

Rawlinson MSS D. 1363, 17th century, Bodleian Library, Oxford

Sloane MSS 3821, 17th century, British Library, London

Sloane MSS 3824, 1649, British Library, London

Sloane MSS 3825, 1641, British Library, London

Printed in July 2019
by Rotomail Italia S.p.A., Vignate (MI) - Italy